55

40¢

DATE DUE

GAYLORD			PRINTED IN U.S.A.

Agricultural Policy and Trade:

Adjusting Domestic Programs in an International Framework

A Task Force Report
to The Trilateral Commission

Authors: D. Gale Johnson, *1916 -*
Professor of Economics,
University of Chicago

Kenzo Hemmi
Former Dean of Faculty of Agriculture,
University of Tokyo;
Chairman of Board,
International Rice Research Institute (IRRI)

Pierre Lardinois
Chairman of Executive Board, Rabobank;
Former Member of Commission of European
Communities;
Former Dutch Minister of Agriculture

Special Consultants: T. K. Warley
Professor of Agricultural Economics,
University of Guelph (Ontario)

P. A. J. Wijnmaalen
Agricultural Counsellor,
Dutch Embassy, Paris

Published by
NEW YORK UNIVERSITY PRESS
New York and London
1985

This report was prepared for the Trilateral Commission and is released under its auspices. It was discussed at the Trilateral Commission meeting in Tokyo on April 21-23, 1985. The authors, who are experts from Western Europe, North America and Japan, have been free to present their own views; and the opinions expressed are put forth in a personal capacity and do not purport to represent those of the Commission or of any organization with which the authors are associated. The Commission is making this report available for wider distribution as a contribution to informed discussion and handling of the issues treated.

The Commission wishes to thank the Robert Bosch Foundation for its generous support of this project.

*

Library of Congress Cataloging-in-Publication Data

Johnson, D. Gale (David Gale), 1916-
　　Agricultural policy and trade.

　　　(Triangle papers ; 29)
　　　1. Agriculture and state—United States. 2. Produce trade—Government policy—
　　United States. 3. United States—Commercial policy. I. Hemmi, Kenzō, 1923-
　　II. Lardinois, Pierre. III. Trilateral Commission. IV. Title. V. Series.
HD1761.J63 1985　　　　　　　　　　338.1'8'0973　　　　　　　　　　85-22264
ISBN 0-8147-4167-3
ISBN 0-8147-4168-1 (pbk.)
　　Manufactured in the United States of America

61,005

The Authors

D. GALE JOHNSON is Eliakim Hastings Distinguished Service Professor of Economics at the University of Chicago. He studied at Iowa State University, the University of Wisconsin, and the University of Chicago; and joined the Chicago faculty in 1944, also serving as Dean (1960-70), as Chairman of the Economics Department (1971-75 and 1981-84), and as Provost of the University (1975-80). Professor Johnson has served as a consultant to the U.S. Agency for International Development, as agricultural advisor of the Office of the President's Special Representative for Trade Negotiations, as a member of the President's National Advisory Committee on Food and Fiber, and on the State Department Policy Planning Council (1967-69). Among his publications are *World Agriculture in Disarray* (1973), *World Food Problems and Prospects* (1975), *Progress of Economic Reform in the People's Republic of China* (1982), and a report to the Trilateral Commission—*Reducing Malnutrition in Developing Countries: Increasing Rice Production in South and Southeast Asia* (1978, with Toshio Shishido and Umberto Colombo).

KENZO HEMMI is Professor of Economics at Asia University in Tokyo and Chairman of the Board of the International Rice Research Institute (IRRI) in the Philippines. After graduating from the University of Tokyo in agricultural economics in 1947, he joined the Japan National Research Institute of Agricultural Economics, which he left in 1961 to join the University of Tokyo faculty, later serving as Dean of the Faculty of Agriculture (1977-81) and Professor (1972-84) until he retired in 1984. Dean Hemmi has been a visiting scholar at the Food Research Institute at Stanford University, a consultant to the United Nations, a Trustee of the Agricultural Development Council, and President of the Asian Association of Agricultural Colleges and Universities (1980-82). Among his publications are: *Nogyo* (Agriculture in the Contemporary Economy, 1970); *Nogyo Seisaku Kogi* (Agricultural Policy, 1971); and *Ajia no Kogyoka to Dai-ichiji Sanpin Kako* (Primary Commodity Exports and Industrialization in Asia, 1975). He was a Special Consultant for the 1978 report to the Trilateral Commission on *Reducing Malnutrition in Developing Countries: Increasing Rice Production in South and Southeast Asia*, and co-editor of *U.S.-Japanese Agricultural Trade Relations* (Resources for the Future, 1982).

PIERRE LARDINOIS is Chairman of the Executive Board of Rabobank Nederland in Utrecht. Educated at the University of Agriculture at

Wageningen, Mr. Lardinois has spent most of his career in public service. From 1951 to 1960, he was National Agricultural Advisor at Eindhoven and subsequently spent three years as Agricultural Attaché with the Dutch Embassy in London. In 1963 he was elected a member of the European Parliament. While a member of the European Parliament, he also became Chairman of the provincial North Brabant Christian Farmers Federation. In 1967 he left both posts to join the Dutch government as Minister for Agriculture and Fisheries, a post he held until 1973. During his last year in the cabinet, he also assumed the portfolio for Surinam and the Netherlands Antilles. From 1973 until joining Rabobank in 1977, Mr. Lardinois was a Member of the Commission of the European Communities (with special responsibility for agriculture).

*   *   *

T.K. WARLEY (Special Consultant) has been Professor of Agricultural Economics at the University of Guelph in Ontario since 1970. Prior to emigrating to Canada in 1970, Prof. Warley was a Reader in Agricultural Economics at the University of Nottingham in Great Britain. In 1970-75, he was Director of the School of Agricultural Economics and Extension Education at the University of Guelph. Prof. Warley has published widely on issues of agricultural policy and trade, and has been associated with agriculture-related assignments for a variety of organizations in North America and Europe.

P.A.J. WIJNMAALEN (Special Consultant) has worked closely with Pierre Lardinois over the years. From 1969 to 1973, he was Director of International Affairs at the Dutch Ministry of Agriculture and Fisheries while Mr. Lardinois was Minister. He was Chef de Cabinet of Mr. Lardinois at the Commission of the European Communities from 1973 to 1977. After several years in the private sector as Director of the Managing Board of an agro-food industrial group in Amsterdam, Mr. Wijnmaalen returned to public service in 1983 as Agricultural Counsellor at the Dutch Embassy in Paris. He is an active participant on the agricultural committees of the OECD and GATT.

The Trilateral Process

The report which follows is the joint responsibility of the three authors, with D. Gale Johnson acting as principal author. Although only the authors are responsible for the analysis and conclusions, they have been aided in their work by many others. The authors would like to express their particular appreciation for the invaluable help of P.A.J. Wijnmaalen and T.K. Warley. Mr. Wijnmaalen has provided vital support throughout the project on the European side. Professor Warley's background paper on Canada—from which the essay in the Appendix has been drawn—was the critical input for the Canadian aspects of this report and some other aspects as well.

The various persons consulted by the authors spoke for themselves as individuals and not as representatives of any institutions with which they are associated. Those consulted or otherwise assisting in the development of the report include the following:

Emmett Barker, *President, Farm & Industrial Equipment Institute, Chicago*

Stewart Borland, *Director-General, Market Analysis and Trade Policy Directorate, Canadian Agriculture Ministry*

Pierre Callebaut, *Chairman, Belgian Federation of Agricultural and Food Industries*

John Campbell, *Professional Staff Member, U.S. Senate Committee on Agriculture*

Takeharu Chikanaga, *Director, Planning Office, Minister's Secretariat, Japanese Ministry of Agriculture, Forestry, and Fisheries*

Norman M. Coats, *Director, Economic Research, Ralston Purina Company*

Philippe Coste, *Head of Policy Planning Staff, French Ministry of External Relations*

Paul Delouvrier, *Chairman of the French Group of the Trilateral Commission*

Pierre Esteva, *Honorary Chairman, Union des Assurances de Paris*

Kenneth Farrell, *Director, National Center for Food & Agricultural Policy, Resources for the Future*

René Foch, *Honorary Director-General, Commission of the European Communities*

Sir Michael Franklin, *Permanent Secretary, Ministry of Agriculture, Fisheries, and Food, United Kingdom*

Robert Frederick, *Legislative Director, National Grange*

Bruce L. Gardner, *Professor of Agricultural Economics, University of Maryland*

Tsutomu Hata, *Member of the Japanese Diet, House of Representatives*

Dale Hathaway, *Vice President, Consultants International Group; former U.S. Undersecretary of Agriculture*

Charles B. Heck, *North American Director, The Trilateral Commission*

Stéphane Hessel, *Ambassadeur de France*

G. William Hoagland, *Deputy Staff Director, U.S. Senate Committee on the Budget*

Takashi Hosomi, *President, Overseas Economic Cooperation Fund*

Tomomitsu Iwakura, *Policy Affairs Research Council, Liberal Democratic Party*

Ivan Jacques, *Assistant Deputy Minister, Marketing & Economics, Canadian Agriculture Ministry*

Hiroshi Peter Kamura, *Senior Staff Member, The Trilateral Commission (Japan)*

Bram J. Kruimel, *Senior Staff Member, Rabobank*

Hideaki Kumazawa, *Director, Planning Division, International Department, Japanese Ministry of Agriculture, Forestry, and Fisheries*

André Lachaux, *Director of Production and Trade, French Ministry of Agriculture*

Dennis Lamb, *Deputy Assistant Secretary, Trade and Commercial Affairs, U.S. Department of State*

Francis Lepâtre, *Chairman, French Federation of Agricultural and Food Industries*

Jacques Lesourne, *Professor, Conservatoire National des Arts et Métiers, Paris*

C. Lockwood Marine, *Senior Vice President, Central Soya Company, Fort Wayne, Indiana*

Leo Mayer, *Associate Administrator, Foreign Agricultural Service, U.S. Department of Agriculture*

Luther C. McKinney, *Senior Vice President, The Quaker Oats Company*

John Mellor, *Director, International Food Policy Research Institute, Washington*

W.N. Miner, *Coordinator, Special Advisory Group on Grains, Ottawa*

Michio Mizoguchi, *Special Advisor (Economic) to the Minister of Foreign Affairs, Japan*

Hyde E. Murray, *Counsel to the Minority, U.S. House of Representatives*

Donald Nelson, *Assistant U.S. Trade Representative for Agriculture and Commodity Policy*

Daniel Newman, *Program Assistant to the North American Director, The Trilateral Commission*

Makito Noda, *Program Officer, Japan Center for International Exchange*

Yoshiji Nogami, *Director, First International Organization Division, Ministry of Foreign Affairs, Japan*

Kazuo Nukazawa, *Director, Financial Affairs Department, Keidanren*

Saburo Okita, *President, International University of Japan; former Foreign Minister*

J.B. Penn, *President, Economic Perspective, Incorporated*

Didier Pineau-Valencienne, *Chairman, Groupe Schneider, Paris*

Paul Révay, *European Director, The Trilateral Commission*

Michel Rocard, *French Minister of Agriculture*

Baron Edmond de Rothschild, *Chairman, Compagnie Financière, Paris*

Gilbert Salomon, *Chairman, SOCOPA, Paris*

Fred Sanderson, *Senior Fellow, Resources for the Future*

John A. Schnittker, *President, Schnittker Associates; former U.S. Undersecretary of Agriculture*

G. Edward Schuh, *Director, Agricultural and Rural Development, World Bank; former Professor of Agriculture and Applied Economics, University of Minnesota*

Sueo Sekiguchi, *Professor of Economics, Osaka University*

Albert Simantov, *Director for Agriculture, Organization for Economic Cooperation and Development*

Robert Thompson, *Senior Staff Economist, U.S. President's Council of Economic Advisers*

Charles Tidbury, *Chairman, Long John International, London*

Nobuhiko Ushiba, *Advisor to the Minister of Foreign Affairs, Japan*

Helmut von Verschuer, *Deputy Director-General for Agriculture, Commission of the European Communities*

James Vertrees, *Principal Analyst, Natural Resources and Commerce Division, Congressional Budget Office*

Takeshi Watanabe, *Japanese Chairman, The Trilateral Commission*

Tadashi Yamamoto, *Japanese Director, The Trilateral Commission*

Clayton K. Yeutter, *President, Chicago Mercantile Exchange; former U.S. Assistant Secretary of Agriculture*

Shigenobu Yoshida, *Director, International Studies Department, National Institute for Research Advancement, Tokyo*

Bonroku Yoshino, *Director, Institute for International Economic Studies, Tokyo*

Michael Yoshitsu, *North American Deputy Director, The Trilateral Commission*

A. de Zeeuw, *Chairman of GATT Committee on Trade in Agriculture*

SCHEDULE OF TASK FORCE ACTIVITIES:

May 1984 — Johnson circulates overall notes on report and particular issues for regional essays.

September 9-10 — Authors meet in Utrecht and consult with European experts. Essays on table concerning agricultural policies in United States, Canada, and Japan.

October 27-29 — Lardinois discusses project with European members of Trilateral Commission during regional meeting in Copenhagen.

December 4 — Johnson discusses partial first draft with U.S. and Canadian experts in Washington.

December 11-12 — Authors meet in Tokyo to discuss partial first draft and consult with Japanese experts. Essay also on table concerning agricultural policy in European Community.

January 1985 — Johnson circulates partial second draft; Lardinois and Hemmi circulate additional materials concerning Europe and Japan.

January 23 — Lardinois meets in Paris with French and other European consultants.

February 4-5 — Authors meet in Washington to discuss partial second draft, to outline and begin drafting final chapter, and to consult with U.S. experts.

March 11 — Full third draft circulated among authors and special consultants.

March 20 — Full draft completed for circulation to Trilateral Commission members.

April 22 — Draft of report discussed at plenary meeting of the Trilateral Commission in Tokyo.

April 21-23 — Authors meet in the wings of Tokyo plenary meeting to discuss final revisions of report.

June — Final revisions of report and appendix elements submitted.

August — Final editing completed.

Table of Contents

Tables and Figures

INTRODUCTION

This is the second Trilateral Commission report focused on agriculture and food. The first was the 1978 report on *Reducing Malnutrition in Developing Countries: Increasing Rice Production in South and Southeast Asia*. That study emphasized the significant potential that existed in the region, with its large and growing population, for increasing per capita food production and reducing the incidence of malnutrition. A number of important measures, including expansion and improvement of irrigation, increasing the availability of modern inputs such as fertilizer, pesticides and herbicides, and improvement of rural institutions, were outlined. Particular emphasis was given to estimating the capital cost of irrigation improvement and expansion and the means were suggested for meeting the capital costs from both international and domestic sources.

While it cannot be said that the specific measures suggested in the task force report have been adopted in full, what can be said is that considerable progress has been made in achieving the objective of doubling rice production in South and Southeast Asia between 1978 and 1993, a span of 15 years. The irrigated area in the region has increased at an annual rate of 1.4 million hectares since the mid-1970s. Rice production in the area was 182 million tons in 1983, an increase of 24 percent in the first third of the period. This is an annual growth rate of 4.4 percent, and very close to the 4.7 percent required for doubling in 15 years.

No claim is made that the Trilateral Commission report was responsible for these positive developments. What is important is that both international and domestic resources have been mobilized to achieve a significant expansion in production of rice and other food crops. Perhaps the most important point of the first Trilateral Commission report on agriculture was that food and nutrition problems have solutions and that, in fact, progress has been and is being made in finding and implementing the solutions.

This report is concerned with a very different set of agricultural issues—adjusting the agricultural policies of the trilateral countries. From an international perspective, these policies leave much to be desired. While our countries have substantially liberalized trade in industrial products over the past four decades, little progress has been made in reducing the barriers to trade in farm products. In all too many cases, particular farm programs—in the European Community, the United States, Canada and Japan—have been devised with little or no concern about their effects upon producers in other countries. Even though GATT rules provide significant exceptions for such products within general prohibitions against quantitative restrictions and export subsidies, most countries have made little or no effort to modify their domestic farm programs to make them consistent with GATT. Agricultural trade issues have been important sources of tension in recent years among trilateral countries—and with other OECD countries (notably Australia and New Zealand) and developing countries as well.

Part of the impetus for our report is provided by the prospect of a new round of multilateral negotiations about agriculture under GATT auspices. The new GATT Round provides an opportunity for progress—and in our final chapter we shall sketch a constructive course for the negotiations. The very essence of new GATT negotiations is to be found in defining the extent to which the pursuit of domestic agricultural policies should be permitted to affect trade by restricting or displacing imports or increasing exports.

It is politically naïve to imagine—as earlier GATT Rounds indicate, for instance—that international undesirability in itself could bring about major agricultural policy changes. These policies have deep internal roots. A more reasonable hope is that as domestic policy regimes are adjusted, these adjustments will move in a direction that makes more international sense. What makes the current moment a relatively propitious one for our report—and provides impetus for our work—is that internal pressures are forcing more serious consideration of agricultural policy adjustments, adjustments which may move in a more market-oriented direction that makes more international sense as well. The most obvious and immediate source of pressure—in all three of our regions—is high government costs of existing arrangements in a tight budget climate.

The policies which concern us here—and are of most concern internationally—are those directly affecting the prices and output of farm products. Chapter I of the report sketches such policies in the United States, Canada, the European Community and Japan. Some of the important differences in the structure of farming in different trilateral regions will be noted, especially since these differences appear to have affected the nature of farm price and income support policies.

The aims of agricultural policies in the three regions are similar. They aim at stabilization of markets, income support, orientation of production and the modernization of farming. Differences among agricultural policies in the three regions are differences of degree rather than of kind. Moreover, domestic agricultural and food policies have always been dominated by national interests and views about the world market. As such they are not very susceptible to negotiation or coordination on a medium term basis. Consequently a more market-oriented stance on international trade has regularly yielded to these imperatives. By their very nature and complexity, agricultural policies with neutral effects on international trade today are non-existent; and there seems to be no accepted standard in the international community to balance the difference in (political) appreciation between "acceptable stabilization of markets" and "unacceptable (income) support." Myths and realities on this issue result in the recurring "diplomacy of the megaphone" or shouting matches across the Atlantic and the Pacific, because the stakes for governments and the farming community are high. The minimum requirement to orient domestic agricultural policies is therefore a trilateral view on the development of "domestic" production and international markets.

Price supports and liberal trade are not in conflict when support levels are set below the trend of international market prices and are adjustable as markets change. Such supports provide a measure of stability—protecting producers against extraordinary temporary price drops—while minimizing market distortion. But price supports are of course often set above international market levels, which then leads to interventions at the border to insulate the internal market—whether through the variable levy typical of the European Community, import quotas used by the United States and Canada, a state-trading agency like that used by Japan for a number of commodities, or some other technique. High price supports have also led governments into the additional problem of dealing with excess supplies. This has happened in all trilateral countries. In the European Community and Japan— traditional large importers among trilateral countries—production of some major commodities, encouraged by high price supports, has grown over time beyond internal consumption. The United States has likewise had high price supports that have generated surpluses of grains and dairy products.[1] One alternative, used at times by all, has been to dispose of excess supplies internationally at subsidized prices.

---

[1] In many developing countries the problem has been just the opposite. Domestic commodity prices have often been held at artificially low levels, with strong adverse effects on domestic food production over time. This report is not about agricultural policies in developing countries, but given the current food crisis in sub-Saharan Africa, the issue cannot be avoided. The second section of Chapter IV briefly discusses the matter somewhat further.

Another alternative is to directly limit internal production—whether through incentives to farmers to take land out of production or, more typically, some form of production quotas, which can lead to remarkable economic distortions. Another alternative, of course, is to induce supply reductions with lower price supports.

Lower budgetary costs do not necessarily mean greater market orientation. Deficiency payment systems, for instance, are probably more market-oriented than price supports in the marketplace at the same target price level; but deficiency payments require much larger budgetary outlays. Price supports shift the costs from taxpayers to consumers.

Chapter II of the report examines the relevant provisions of GATT. It draws together available work on the trade effects of the programs laid out in Chapter I, including effects on developing countries. The OECD is now engaged in a remarkably comprehensive assessment along these lines, but that work was not available in time for use in this report—we hope it will be available for the new GATT Round. Chapter II (and Section E of the Appendix) includes an examination of effects of agricultural policies on the level and stability of international prices— which we do by presenting some of the existing research on what would happen to the level and stability of international prices if there were reduction in protection. Current policies tend to increase the instability of international prices. Greater international price variations are a necessary corollary of policies which eliminate internal price variations through varying imports in line with fluctuations in domestic production. As for the level of prices, some international markets are so distorted—such as sugar and dairy products—that it is virtually impossible to gauge the price effects of market-oriented domestic policies; but in both of these cases international price levels would probably rise considerably. In other major markets where analysis is more feasible, market-oriented policies would not have marked effects. Except for rice, the general effect would be to increase prices somewhat. Part of the analytical argument of our report is that if the trilateral countries acted in unison to reduce their market interventions, the presumed adverse effects of liberalization would be significantly reduced. International prices would become more stable, at roughly the same or higher levels for most major commodities.

There would of course be costs in moving to more market-oriented agricultural policies. Chapter III notes three kinds of transition costs: short run losses in farm income, the loss in value of assets and the costs of adjustment to alternative employment for those farmers who must leave agriculture as protection is removed or substantially reduced.

These costs are real and if there is to be any realistic chance of liberalization, these costs must be recognized and compensatory measures taken. While there would be short run income losses in the move to more market-oriented policies, we believe that the long run effect of the removal of trade interventions and other protective measures upon the return to labor and capital employed in agriculture would be negligible provided that there are opportunities for farm workers to find attractive non-farm employment. This is true because the protective measures are ineffective in increasing over time the returns to any resource engaged in agriculture, other than farm land. There is ample evidence that income transfers in the United States quickly become capitalized into the value of assets in inelastic supply (e.g., land), enriching their first generation recipients but leaving their successors with higher entry barriers and a dangerously burdensome cost structure—and increasing the cost of adjustment to more market-oriented policies.

As we shall emphasize with both vigor and conviction, the prospects for changing the current domestic agricultural programs to market-oriented policies will be greatly enhanced if the macroeconomic policies in the trilateral countries provide for employment conditions that make it relatively easy for farm men and women to find non-farm jobs when farm employment provides inadequate incomes. We cannot expect farm people to accept more market-oriented policies unless there are non-farm job opportunities of an attractive nature available.

It must also be recognized that there are substantial differences among geographic regions in the ease with which adjustments can be made. For example, in the farm communities in northern Europe the differences between the country and the city have diminished. In the past when conditions of reasonably full employment prevailed, farm people could more easily adjust to changing economic conditions affecting agriculture, including policy changes. But in southern Europe the differences between country and city remain quite large and farm people find it more costly and difficult to adjust to changing conditions. It is necessary to recognize that such differences do exist and that it is desirable to undertake special measures to promote adjustments.

The average income of farm families in each of our regions has risen significantly during the postwar era as a percentage of average family income in the overall economy. The improvement in income, however, has come in part from the increase in income from non-farm sources—such income now constitutes more than half of the income of farm families in our countries. This is an indication of the integration of farm people over time into the general economy as a consequence of improved education, transportation, and communication. One result of increased integration and non-farm employment possibilities has been the increase in part-time farms as a percentage of all farms, and for these farms the effects of farm price policies on their incomes is much less than for full-time farms. The basic analytical point here is a simple one, but not generally understood: The average incomes of all farm families are determined more by the levels of income in the economy generally than by the level of farm prices or by changes in farm prices over an extended period of time.

The level of farm prices does determine to some degree how many people will be engaged in agriculture, which leads us to another basic analytical point reflected in the postwar economic history of all of our countries: The process of economic growth everywhere requires that the absolute level of employment in agriculture decline over time. Farm employment must decline given the combination of low income elasticity of demand for farm products (i.e., demand increases more slowly than income in our countries) with productivity change at least as rapid as in the rest of the economy. In fact increases in labor productivity in agriculture have generally been greater than in industrial employment. No country has been able to avoid the decline in farm employment, and attempts to do so become quite costly to taxpayers or consumers. We recognize the presence in each of our societies of disadvantaged, often older rural persons with a claim on society for assistance, but this assistance is better provided—at less cost to the overall community— through targeted programs rather than through high agricultural price supports that generally benefit other producers more.

Whatever its analytical merits, we recognize that general liberalization is not politically feasible in the near future. But progress can and should be made toward more market-oriented policies, toward lower levels of protection. In our final chapter—Chapter IV—we set out high priority adjustments for the United States, Canada, the European Community and Japan. While we are aware of the immediate policy debates in each of our regions, we have not let ourselves be completely bound by immediate political constraints. It is our purpose to look a little further down the road at those high priority adjustments which can and should be made over the medium term.

It is quite clear what is required if domestic farm policy regimes are to contribute to an improved international situation for all producers and consumers. We recommend that domestic programs should be made more market-oriented; that the trilateral countries should move together in achieving more market-oriented policies for agriculture; that it should be recognized that it is not possible to move to more market-oriented policies all at once; and that during the transition period there should be no additional trade barriers introduced nor should existing barriers be unilaterally broadened.

New GATT Round negotiations on agriculture provide an important framework for multilateral progress over the next several years, and in Chapter IV we also try to set out a constructive path for these negotiations. We have not approached this effort in the spirit of negotiators for our individual countries or regions. The spirit here, as throughout this report, has been that of a joint effort to help us all move forward. We all stand to gain from more market-oriented agricultural policies that make more international sense.

Our report is in two parts. The main body of the report is a relatively short statement of the main points and conclusions that we have reached concerning the reasons why domestic farm programs need to be changed and our views concerning how these policies could be gradually modified to create the conditions for smoother international relations among the trilateral countries and between the trilateral countries and the developing countries.

An Appendix provides background and support for the policy-oriented main body. The Appendix also includes a significant amount of descriptive material that we believe those who wish to become acquainted with the major agricultural policy and trade issues confronting the trilateral countries will find helpful. The main body is written to be self-contained, though it is our hope that some will find the material in it sufficiently interesting to induce turning to the Appendix as well.

I. Domestic Farm Programs

Governmental intervention in agricultural pricing, exporting, financing and output decisions is evident in each of the trilateral countries. True, there are differences in degree among our countries, but no government can say that it follows market-oriented policies to such an extent that it can everywhere permit reasonably free flow of farm products across its borders.

There are differences in the specific price support and income measures used by various governments. Some measures impose most of the costs upon consumers while others place the burden more upon taxpayers. But the effects—creation of excess or undesired production and interference with the reasonably free flow of trade—are similar. In this chapter we present very short summaries of the farm price support and income policies of the United States, Canada, the European Community and Japan. These policies are discussed in greater detail in the Appendix to our report.

The summaries that we present here cover only those policies that have a direct effect upon trade in agricultural products. We include primarily those measures directly affecting the prices of farm products in national markets or that encourage farm production through subsidies that are related to current production. Governments have many other programs that affect agricultural production, such as research, education, social security, and inspectional services, but these are measures that have broad social purposes and often are the same as or similar to measures affecting other parts of the economy.

We are critical of the market intervention features of the agricultural policies of the trilateral countries. These policies impose substantial costs upon consumers and taxpayers. Further, it has become increasingly evident that the programs are not cost effective in terms of their objectives.

Internationally, the programs have been sources of conflict and misunderstanding among the trilateral countries. The methods used to increase farm incomes and achieve food security have resulted in creating farm surpluses with adverse effects upon the developing countries and other low cost producers that depend upon agricultural exports for foreign exchange earnings.

However, we would like to stress that overall agricultural policies have had many positive results as well. These policies have improved agricultural productivity and modernization. To some considerable degree the present problems of excess production capacities and unwanted supplies have been due to the remarkable increases in agricultural productivity over the past quarter century. The agricultural policies of the trilateral countries have given the farmers the incentives to produce in abundance. This is in sharp contrast to the effects of the agricultural policies of the Soviet Union and most of Eastern Europe, where farm production has lagged significantly behind demand. Except for Hungary, the Communist countries of Europe have had to rely upon imports to supply a significant percentage of their food supplies. Within little more than a decade, the Soviet Union has changed from a net exporter of food and other agricultural products to become one of the two or three largest importers of food in the world.[1]

Consequently while we believe that the farm price and income support programs of the trilateral countries can be improved—in the long run benefitting virtually everyone, including most farmers—we fully recognize that the whole mix of agricultural policies has had several positive results. Combined with the ingenuity of our farmers, they are now providing us with more food than ever before for the smallest percentage of our living expenditures that has ever been achieved. While consumers in our countries are now paying more for their food than they would under more market-oriented policies, the percentage of their consumption expenditures spent on food is at an all-time low of 20 percent in the European Community, 16 percent in the United States, 16 percent in Canada and 24 percent in Japan. Just two decades ago consumers in these countries were allocating a significantly higher percentage of their consumption expenditures on food.

The farm programs of the trilateral countries have not significantly slowed the reduction in employment in agriculture, an adjustment that is required by economic growth. Between 1960 and 1979 farm employment in the European Community, Japan, Canada, and the United States declined from 39.2 million to 21.4 million . This was a decline of 44 percent. And as shall be shown later the rate of decline in the farm

---

[1]The dependence of the Centrally Planned Economies upon imports of agricultural products is now very great. In the early 1980s these economies accounted for a third of world imports of grain. But grain is not all that is imported; these economies import a sixth of the world's trade in all agricultural products. These economies pose some problems in trade since all of their trade occurs through state-trading agencies. While our report does not deal with the particular issues that arise in trading that is so conducted, it would seem to be in the interests of the trilateral countries to consider if there are ways in which the trading relations with the CPEs in farm products might be improved and conducted in a manner that served the interests of farmers in the trilateral countries.

labor force was as great in the countries with relatively high prices as it was in those with lower farm prices. The dynamic characteristics of modern agriculture were clearly not inhibited by the farm price and income policies. As further evidence of this, over and above the declining relative cost of food and the large transfer of labor from agriculture to the non-farm sectors of our economies, between 1960 and 1980 labor productivity in agriculture increased at a somewhat higher rate than in manufacturing. In only one country—Japan—did the growth of labor productivity in manufacturing exceed that of agriculture by a significant margin. In the EC-9 countries (i.e., without Greece, Spain, and Portugal) labor productivity rose from 1968 to 1975 by an annual average of about 3.1 percent, while the annual increase for agriculture was 6.3 percent. Also, in the period 1975 to 1980 the figure for agriculture was more than double. In both Canada and the United States labor productivity growth in agriculture was greater than in manufacturing.

In sum, the agricultural achievements of the trilateral countries are real and substantial. The cost of food has been reduced as a component of consumer budgets, agricultural productivity has increased at a rapid pace, most of the adjustments in farm employment required by economic growth have now occurred, and the degree of food security has been enhanced with the great expansion of international trade in agricultural products in the past two decades. But much can be done to improve the cost effectiveness of these programs and reduce tension among the nations that import and export agricultural products. It is the purpose of our report to suggest ways of improving the cost effectiveness of farm programs through realizing the benefits of more market-oriented programs.

A. UNITED STATES AGRICULTURAL POLICY

As this is written, the U.S. Congress is in the midst of debating new omnibus farm legislation, a quadrennial exercise in the United States. Current price and income programs are primarily based upon the Food and Agricultural Act of 1981. That legislation provided minimum price support levels for 1982 through 1985 for wheat, feed grains, soybeans, dairy products, peanuts, and sugar. The soybean price support was set at a level expected to be below actual market prices and this has proved to be the case. The same cannot be said about the other price supports, however.

In the cases of wheat, feed grains, rice, and cotton the price supports are in the form of nonrecourse loans. Under a nonrecourse loan, a farmer obtains a loan at a specified level on the amount of his wheat or corn or rice that he pledges as security. The ordinary loan is for a period of less than a year. At the time the loan becomes due, the farmer has the right to pay off the loan with interest and recover his security (the farm product pledged) or to deliver the farm product to the government and have the loan cancelled. He chooses the second alternative when the market price is below the loan rate. It is the loan rate that sets the minimum price of the market, and in the case of grains, significantly influences the level of the minimum world market prices. It is the decisions made by farmers concerning the delivery of their pledged products that keep the market price at or very near the loan or support price.

A second important feature of U.S. price policy is the target price. The target price does not directly affect the market price but is used to determine a deficiency payment, which is equal to the difference between the target price on one hand and, on the other, the market price or loan rate, whichever is the higher. The target prices can and do influence farmers' production decisions. If target prices are set significantly above what market prices would be in the absence of governmental intervention, then output is increased.

The deficiency payments are not automatically available to all farmers. Farmers are required to participate in supply management programs to receive them. However, in some years the acreage limitations were modest and had little effect in reducing production. In the 1980s only the massive Payment-in-Kind (PIK) Program in 1983—under which, in return for reducing acreage, farmers were paid in kind a high percentage of their normal yields—had a significant impact upon crop production. The PIK program was instituted to reduce the available stocks of grain and cotton, to strengthen market prices, and to lower governmental costs for storage and deficiency payments.

Dairy prices are supported by direct purchases by the Agriculture Department's Commodity Credit Corporation of manufactured milk products—principally butter, cheese, and dry skim milk. The purchase prices for dairy products are significantly above international market prices. Consequently, it is necessary that imports be strictly limited. This is done through the use of import quotas, for which the United States obtained a waiver in 1955 in the General Agreement on Tariffs and Trade (GATT). The waiving of GATT obligations was necessary in that the price support program for dairy products violated the conditions under which the use of quantitative restrictions was permissible. It was not until 1984 that the United States made any effort to restrict the production of dairy products and thus to potentially bring its use of dairy import quotas into compliance with Article XI of GATT.

The United States supports sugar prices presumably through a price support program but in fact by strict limitations over the importation of sugar. Before 1974 there was an effort to limit sugar production in the United States, but since import controls were reinstituted in 1978 there has been no limitation on domestic sugar production. Domestic sugar prices are substantially above world market prices and sufficiently high to encourage the production of high fructose sugar from corn and thus further reduce the imports of sugar.

The Agricultural Act of 1981 set price supports that at the time were believed to be at reasonable levels. Of course, subsequent events showed this to have been an erroneous belief. At the time it was believed that world demand for farm products would grow at a more rapid rate than supply. Instead the contrary occurred and the farm price supports set in the 1981 Act resulted in the accumulation of large stocks in the hands of the government. An important defect of the 1981 Act was that it established minimum levels for both target prices and loan levels and made no provision for downward adjustments if the assumptions about demand and supply conditions were incorrect, as was the case.

Congress was unwilling to recognize its mistake until 1984 when legislation was passed permitting modest downward adjustments of two percent to five percent in target prices for wheat for 1984 and 1985. Reductions of similar magnitudes were made in the target prices for corn and cotton for 1985. No changes were made in the target prices for barley, grain sorghums, and oats. The 1985 target price for rice was frozen at the 1984 level.

The relationships between target prices and loan rates for the various commodities have been far from uniform. In 1983, when the relationships were those set in the 1981 Act, the target price for wheat was 33 percent greater than the loan rate and for rice 40 percent greater, while for corn the difference was just eight percent. For cotton the difference was 38 percent. The target prices for wheat, rice and cotton had the clear effect of influencing farmers' production decisions and helped to retain excess resources in agriculture.

As noted above, the target prices and loan rates are not automatically available to each farmer. To obtain these benefits, farmers must participate in supply management programs. The supply management programs have resulted in idling or diverting substantial amounts of cropland in some years. The diversions have been very large in some years, such as 1972 and 1983. However, the supply management programs have not resulted in eliminating the excess productive capacity of U.S. agriculture.

Soybeans have not been included in the supply management programs. This has been true, at least in part, because the price supports for soybeans have been at levels that have seldom resulted in any significant accumulation of soybean stocks—thus making them the most market-oriented of major U.S. price supports.

There are no price supports for beef, pork, or poultry and eggs. Imports of beef and veal are covered by voluntary export controls by the major exporters—Australia and New Zealand. Imports of cooked beef, primarily from Latin America, are not restricted.

For the past decade the United States has not made significant use of explicit export subsidies. Food aid, which involves providing food at less than market prices, constitutes a type of export subsidy. However, since the mid-1970s the annual volume of food aid under Public Law 480 has accounted for less than five percent of all agricultural exports. There was, of course, the highly publicized sale of wheat flour to Egypt in 1983 by the use of a large export subsidy; and the United States has used credit subsidies as a means of increasing commercial exports. Except for exports as a part of food aid, the U.S. surplus of dairy products has been disposed of in the domestic market.

B. CANADIAN AGRICULTURAL POLICY

Canada has a program of price floors. They apply to nine commodities (beef cattle, hogs, sheep and lambs, industrial milk and cream, corn, soybeans, oats, and barley grown outside the designated area of the Canadian Wheat Board) and are set at not less than 90 percent of the average market prices over the previous five years, adjusted by the difference between unit production costs in the current year and average production costs in the previous five-year reference period. The price floors are technically similar to target prices in the United States since the floors are used to determine the size of deficiency payments if the market price falls below that level; but they are also quite different than U.S. target prices in being set so low. Actual payments to producers of products other than industrial milk and cream have been sporadic and variable.

In Canada the provincial governments have a significant role in farm programs. The federal Agricultural Stabilization Act (ASA), except for milk, has been market-oriented and stabilizing in intent and has been designed to be neutral with respect to resource use and the marketing of farm products. However, producers and the provincial governments have judged the federal benefits to be too modest. Provincial governments have introduced a wide variety of ad hoc support payments or ongoing commodity stabilization programs for producers in their provinces. For non-dairy commodities, expenditures on provincial stabilization programs averaged $74 million annually between 1974/75 and 1982/83, i.e., 50 percent more than federal expenditures under the ASA in the same period. While the federal programs have been designed with concern for the effects of such measures upon international trade, the provinces appear not to have given any significant attention to trade implications.

The federal government's Western Grains Stabilization Act of 1976 provides an income insurance program for producers in the designated area of the Canadian Wheat Board. Producers are assured that if their net cash flow falls below the average of the previous five years, a payment equal to the shortfall is made for the year. This is a voluntary program and producers must contribute to a stabilization fund an amount equal to two percent of their gross receipts. The federal government contributes two dollars for every dollar paid by the producers. Payments under the program have been infrequent and modest. The benefits have been so modest that consideration is being given to providing producers with larger and more timely benefits in periods of economic difficulties. Even so, it is likely that the program will continue to be a stabilization program rather than a support program.

The Canadian Wheat Board—a state-trading agency—announces and pays initial prices for the grain and oilseed products for which it has a marketing monopoly. While the initial prices are guaranteed by the federal government, these prices are set cautiously and in relation to anticipated world prices. The total payments to producers for their crops depend upon the actual returns from the sale of a particular year's production. Taxpayer costs to implement the guarantee have been rare and small.

The price support programs for dairy and poultry products cannot be described as market-oriented. Fluid milk pricing and marketing is under provincial control. In each province, producers' marketing boards price fluid milk on the basis of calculated "full" costs of production. Aggregate output is limited by producer quotas to make supply equal to demand at the set price. Little milk crosses provincial boundaries and none can be imported from the United States. Industrial milk policy is based on a target price. It is implemented by a fixed subsidy or deficiency payment and by purchases by the government. The domestic price is maintained by quantitative restrictions on imports of manufactured dairy products, by restrictions on the importation and use of dairy substitutes, and by disposing of excess dry skim milk by export at subsidized prices. The market value of the milk quotas has reached very large figures. The value or price of the milk quota for the output of one cow was approximately $4,500 (Canadian) in the province of Ontario in 1984. This is substantially more than the price of a highly productive dairy cow.

Egg and poultry price supports and marketing arrangements are similar to those for dairy products. Producer prices are set by formula to equal full production costs and aggregate output is controlled to equal the amount demanded at those prices. Output shares or quotas are allocated to each producer and imports are controlled to prevent lower cost imports from entering the market. No direct subsidies are paid by governments; consumers pay the full cost of the programs through prices that are normally much higher than in the United States. As in the case of milk quotas, the quotas for eggs, broilers, and turkeys are valuable and costly assets. In Ontario in 1984, the market value of the quota for eggs was $30 (Canadian) for a laying hen; for turkeys the market value of one bird was about $14 (Canadian). The import quotas for poultry products reflect the historic share of imports in Canadian consumption and are thus considered to be in conformity with GATT Article XI.

C. AGRICULTURAL POLICIES
OF THE EUROPEAN COMMUNITY

A key element of the European Community is the Common Agricultural Policy though it is not the sole component. The CAP is not uniform over all commodities for which there is a common market organization. However, for about three fourths of EC production there is a system of support prices. The commodities covered include most cereals, sugar, milk, beef and veal, pork, certain fruits and vegetables, and table wine. For most of the remaining agricultural production the market organizations are primarily in the form of border protection without specific internal price support operations. For more precise information, see Section C of the Appendix.

The CAP for cereals starts from target prices set annually by the Council of Agriculture Ministers of the European Community. The actual prices received by farmers are determined by two other prices which, while related to the target price, are significantly below it. One is the threshold price; the other is the intervention price.

The threshold price determines the price at which imports are permitted to enter the Community. If the world market price is below the threshold price, a variable levy equal to the difference is imposed. The threshold price is less than the target price by the cost of unloading and transporting the product to major consuming centers.

If domestic supply exceeds demand, the actual producer price will be below the target price. If the producer price falls far enough, the intervention price comes into play. The Community is committed to purchase products offered to it at the intervention price.

When Community producers export, they are refunded the difference between the market price in the Community (including transport costs to the port of export) and the selling price on the world market. If the world market price is greater than the threshold price, imports are subsidized—in order to keep the domestic price from increasing above the target price—and exports are taxed. This happened for wheat, barley, maize and sugar at various times from 1973 to 1975.

For poultry and pigmeat the variable levy has two components: a first part matches the difference between the world price of cereals and the EC price to offset the difference between internal and external feed costs, and a second part is equal to seven percent of the sluice-gate price. The sluice-gate price is the estimated cost price of pigmeat, poultrymeat and eggs in the non-member countries with the highest technical efficiency. The second part is clearly designed to provide protection for pork and poultry producers.

A very important objective of the Common Agricultural Policy has been to have the same prices, subject only to differences in transport costs, prevail throughout the Community. However, exchange rates have varied over time and this has resulted in departures from common prices. When a country revalues its currency, a common price policy would require that the agricultural prices of the country be changed to reflect the revaluation. Prices in the domestic currency should be reduced by the percentage that the exchange rate increased. If there were a devaluation, farm prices in domestic currencies ought to be raised. Such changes have not been politically acceptable and the system of handling the national price differences that resulted was one of "green rates" and Monetary Compensation Amounts. The MCAs were applied to trade among member countries in such a way as to permit member countries to have domestic prices that were either higher or lower than would have prevailed if the official exchange rates had been used to set domestic prices.

The CAP is financed from the European Agricultural Guidance and Guarantee Fund (EAGGF). The EAGGF has accounted for over 70 percent of Community expenditures in a number of years. Import levies and levies paid by some producer groups, such as sugar and dairy, are used to finance a part of the total expenditures. The Guidance part of the fund is used to finance the Community's contributions for structural programs. The primary objective of structural policy is to minimize regional variations in the economic prospects of farm people by helping the disadvantaged regions to improve their economic viability.

The various price supports, protection systems and producer aids have generally been applied to unlimited amounts of production and have contributed (in varying degrees according to the product) to substantial increases in agricultural production, resulting in surpluses in some cases. To deal with surpluses and the political difficulties of reducing them by cutting producer prices substantially, steps have been taken to limit the guarantees offered. In some cases, certain amounts of production have been excluded from guarantees—by fixing guarantee thresholds, by limiting the resources used, or by making producers responsible for the cost of marketing the surpluses they produce.

Some examples of the above efforts to limit the surpluses that would otherwise be generated by high prices may be noted. There are three different prices for sugar—a high price for sugar used within the EC, a lower price for sugar which can be sold on favorable terms to non-member countries, and the world price for sugar that must be exported on the open market. The producer receives individual quotas covering the first two categories of sugar; he is free to produce as much of the surplus sugar as desired but without expectation of any subsidy. The sugar scheme is without cost to the EC governments, with the financial costs of surplus disposal being paid by the levies assessed against the producers. The full implementation of this scheme has resulted in a decline in sugar production. In contrast to the United States, the EC strictly limits the production of high fructose sugar. Consequently there has been less displacement of beet and cane sugar by sugar produced from corn.

The EC dairy policy was changed in 1984 by the introduction of quotas assigned to individual producers. The objective was to reduce milk production by 4.25 percent in the first year (1984/85).

For cereals the commitment to support prices is no longer a completely open-ended one but is for a threshold amount. Cereal prices are to be related to a three-year average of production. If such production exceeds the threshold amount, prices will be lowered.

As a relatively high guaranteed price is always applied to a fairly large proportion of the quantity produced and as farmers are influenced in their production decisions by the average price they expect to

receive, these measures do not stop the production of unwanted surpluses. At the same time, they may reduce the incentive to produce
more than a certain amount. In this way, the measures can have a
positive direct effect on trade to the extent that they prevent the growth
of surpluses and the export of large quantities to outside markets.

D. AGRICULTURAL POLICY IN JAPAN

Present agricultural policy consists of two groups of programs; one
originating in agrarian Japan and the other in developed Japan. The
Staple Food Control Program of 1942, the Land Reform Program of 1946
and the Agricultural Cooperative Program of 1948 belong to the former
group. When these were launched primary industry formed about a
quarter of Japan's gross national product and employed about half of
her total labor force. Food was in severe short supply, and consumers
were spending more than half of their total consumption expenditure
on food. After 1955 both the agricultural and non-agricultural economies were reconstructed from the war damage, and food shortages
had disappeared. Adjustment to the growing Japanese economy became the central agricultural problem. Programs under the Basic Agricultural Act of 1961 form the second group. The 1961 Act was designed
to increase productivity of labor in agriculture by improving the basic
structure of the agricultural sector, to adjust agricultural production to
the changing demand situation, and to reduce the number of farms.
The goal was one million "viable" farms by 1970, whose average productivity would yield the farmer the equivalent of an urban worker in
income. This meant that at least 1.2 million farmers, out of a total of 6
million, would have to leave farming in ten years.

Although the programs of the 1940s (especially the Staple Food
Control Program) have adjusted to the growing Japanese economy
since 1955, the basic structure of these programs has been maintained
to today. These aim at encouraging as many mini-size owner-operators
as possible to remain in farming and at producing as much output as
technologically possible, while the latter group of programs, as we
have noted, emphasizes assuring fair income to the farmers by increasing farm productivity and supporting agricultural prices.

Japanese agricultural policy over the years has swung between the
poles of increasing food supplies (or food security) and increasing
productivity (or production in line with comparative advantage).
When foods are in abundant supply both domestically and internationally, increasing productivity is stressed. Thus, from 1960 to 1973,
policy emphasized increasing productivity. When food is in tight sup-

ply, price support is stressed to increase domestic production. Thus, with the 1973 "grain crisis"—especially the soybean embargo by the United States—and the establishment of a 200-mile fishing zone in many of the world's waters, the emphasis shifted towards increasing food supply.

From 1980 the policy has gradually swung toward increasing produc‑ tivity again. The Government's "Basic Guidelines of Government Agri‑ cultural Policy in 1980," published in November 1980, will guide Japanese agricultural policy for several more years. There are two themes to the guidelines. One is the maintenance of current Japanese food consumption patterns. The present level and pattern of Japanese food consumption is said to be ideal for human health. Moreover, to maintain the present level and pattern of Japanese food consumption is considered to be desirable for the nation's food security. The con‑ servative attitude of the government toward significant increases in meat consumption stems from this view of Japan's food consumption pattern. This view explains why the government is so strict in demand‑ ing complete self-sufficiency in rice, and why the government is so adamant in asserting that future Japanese meat consumption will not be much above the present level.

The second theme of the 1980 "Basic Guidelines of Government Agricultural Policy" is the adoption of the target of increasing Japanese agricultural productivity to the level of EC countries. The government had been very disappointed with the poor results of the Basic Agri‑ cultural Program of 1961. At the end of 1970, instead of there being one million "viable" farms—representing the projected 20.6 percent of all farms—the percentage of "viable" to total farms had decreased from 8.6 percent in 1960 to 6.6 percent in 1970 (and it declined further to 5.2 percent in 1980). In 1973, the government shifted its policy from en‑ couraging "viable" farms to encouraging "responsible" farms (at least one male farm worker younger than 60 years old and working 150 days or more on his farm annually), which were to be responsible for the healthy growth of Japanese agriculture. These "responsible" farms made up one third of total farms and produced two thirds of the sector's output in 1973. Judging from their age distribution, an increas‑ ing number of Japanese farmers will be retiring in the near future. They have to transfer their agricultural lands to other, younger farmers. Therefore, there will be increasing possibilities for these younger farm‑ ers to enlarge their farms. This is the background for the idea of playing catch-up with EC agriculture. According to the government's target for the program, declared in 1982, there will be 700,000 "responsible" farms in 1990 (comprising 17 percent of total Japanese farms and using

60 percent of total arable land), decreasing to 400,000 by 2000. The government has been stern in trying not to raise nominal producers' prices of various farm products during the past several years. It expects that Japanese support levels will finally converge with EC support levels since it was expected that the EC would have to increase its support prices. The high level of support for agriculture in Japan has increasingly been criticized by exporters, and EC support levels offer a convenient target.

Japanese agricultural policy is characterized by very high levels of price supports, shown in Table 1, which have increased steadily during the past 25 years. Japanese support levels were actually lower than those of EC countries in 1955. They were almost the same as those of EC countries in 1960, and much higher than those of EC countries in 1970. The increase was caused by both increases in domestic support prices of the commodities concerned and by changes in the exchange rate of the yen *vis-à-vis* European currencies. Another trend evident in Table 1 is that support levels for grains were always much higher than for

TABLE 1

Levels of Agricultural Price Supports in Japan, 1955-80
(percent)

		1955	1960	1965	1970	1975	1980
13 Products[a]	PSR[d]	15.0	29.3	40.3	42.1	42.7	45.5
	NRP[e]	17.6	41.4	67.5	72.7	74.5	83.5
Grains[b]	PSR	19.5	33.1	49.2	57.4	55.2	66.2
	NRP	24.2	49.5	96.9	134.7	123.2	195.9
Livestock	PSR	−8.5	18.1	20.4	19.0	27.3	28.7
Products[c]	NRP	−7.8	22.1	25.6	23.5	37.6	40.3

[a]Weighted average of wheat, rye, barley, oats, maize, rice, sugar beet, potatoes, beef, pork, chicken, eggs and milk.

[b]Weighted average of wheat, rye, barley, oats, maize and rice.

[c]Weighted average of beef, pork, chicken, eggs and milk.

[d]Producer Support Ratio (PSR) is the ratio to the *domestic* price of the price difference between the domestic price and the border price.

[e]Nominal Rate of Protection (NRP) is the ratio to the *border* price of the price difference between the domestic price and the border price.

Source: Yujiro Hayami and Masayoshi Honma, *Agricultural Protection Level of Japan* (Tokyo: Forum for Policy Innovation, November 1983, in Japanese).

livestock products. There are two reasons for this difference. The main reason is that Japanese farmers have generally fed animals and chickens with imported feeds. (Therefore, the levels in Table 1 do not show the effective rate of protection for livestock at all.) The second reason is that high government rice price supports—the largest portion of the weighted average for grains—have never been severely criticized, either by rice exporting countries or by Japanese consumers. In a number of rice exporting countries rice prices are held below international market levels. If there were liberalization, rice consumption would fall and rice production would increase in these countries. Therefore, the status quo in the world rice market is considered by some to be good for these countries. The third trend in Table 1 is that support levels for livestock products did increase from 1970 to 1975 while support levels for grains did not increase in the same period. During this period prices of livestock products were marked up along with the increases in prices of imported feeds.

The rice surplus has dominated the whole range of Japan's agricultural policies in recent years. Three successive good crops from 1967 to 1969 culminated in 7.2 million tons of stock in 1970, the disposal of which cost the government 1,000 billion yen. In addition to surplus disposal, the government had to divert about 14 percent of the total paddy rice acreage in 1971-75 and about 23 percent of it in 1978-82 into other crops. Since rice is a sacred commodity in Japan, and production of it was most profitable among crops produced in Japan at that time, the government had to pay not only diversion payments but also various kinds of subsidies to encourage a shift toward non-rice crops (such as wheat, soybeans, fodder crops, and so on) on paddy fields. One effect of the rice diversion program was the increase in wheat production from 1977. Another effect was the increase in the level of grain price supports from 1975 to 1980, as shown in Table 1. These and other effects of the crop diversion programs retarded (and will retard) the swing of Japan's agricultural policy from the pole of increasing food supplies to the pole of increasing productivity significantly.

The government support (price stabilization) programs have covered about 70 percent of total agricultural production. (A major exception is fruit, none of which is subject to price support measures.) In many cases the support levels are determined annually by very detailed (rigid) formulas such as a parity formula (wheat and barley), a cost of production plus compensation formula (rice), etc. This necessitates various kinds of intervention.

Ad valorem duties are less preferred than other forms of intervention at the border because *ad valorem* duties are less effective in isolating domestic support prices from price fluctuations in the world market. Beside moderate import duties, the following government interventions are presently used in connection with price supports of various commodities. Rice, wheat, flour, barley, sterilized fresh milk and cream, condensed milk, butter, and tobacco leaves are subject to state-trading. Beef, oranges, processed cheese, peanuts, and some juices (including orange juice) are subject to quota systems (residual quantitative import restrictions). Sugar is subject to a variable levy system that works when the c.i.f. price is lower than a certain level. Maize for non-feeding purposes is subject to a tariff quota system. Pork, ham, and bacon are subject to sliding tariff rates. Soybeans, sugar, rapeseeds, and milk for processing are subject to deficiency payment systems.

E. CONSUMER AND TAXPAYER COSTS[2]

We indicated earlier our conclusion that the domestic farm programs of the trilateral countries involve large costs and are no longer cost effective. What are the costs of the farm programs? This is not a simple question to answer, in part because costs are of several kinds. Here we shall address but one concept of cost, namely the costs that the price and income support programs impose upon taxpayers and consumers. The details underlying our estimates may be found in the Appendix of this report.

There is no simple way to calculate the costs to taxpayers and consumers of the agricultural price and income support programs. The major problem in estimating consumer costs is the determination of what international market prices would be if the OECD countries and some of the rapidly growing developing countries followed market-oriented agricultural policies with little or no protection for their agricultures. In Chapter II and the Appendix we present the results of studies that have estimated the magnitude of the distortions in world market prices of several important farm products due to the prevailing interventions in international trade in agricultural products. The estimated depressing effects of these policies for the grains and meat are relatively small, perhaps 10 percent or somewhat more; however, for dairy products and sugar the price distortions are much greater. In our

---

[2]The European author does not believe that taxpayer and consumer costs, as they are presented in this section, are adequate measures for evaluating agricultural policies in our three regions. The reason is that in many cases the so-called world market prices are no usable alternative to calculate this kind of cost. Moreover, the advantages, such as those of stable food supply, are not taken into account; and there are many other costs and volume effects to deal with.

TABLE 2

Costs to Consumers and Taxpayers of Agricultural Support Programs in Canada, Japan and the United States, 1979/80 and 1982/83[a]

	CANADA	JAPAN[b]	UNITED STATES
	(million US$)		
1979/80			
Excess Consumer Costs	1,451	9,760	8,406
Taxpayer Costs	1,049	5,923	3,833[c]
Total	2,500	15,683	12,239
1982/83			
Excess Consumer Costs		8,265	13,166
Taxpayer Costs		4,728	19,220[c]
Total		12,990	32,386
	(percent)		
Total costs as percent of value of domestic use at world prices			
1979/80	21	62	18
1982/83		51	49

Note: Supporting tables for the Japan and United States columns are to be found in the Appendix (Tables US-9 and JN-3). The Canadian figure for excess consumer costs is a 1980 figure derived from Table CN-5 in the Appendix, calculated by subtracting farm cash receipts at border prices from farm cash receipts at domestic prices—1,702 million Canadian dollars. The Canadian taxpayer cost figure—1,230.4 million Canadian dollars—is taken from Appendix Table CN-4 and is a 1980/81 figure. These numbers were then converted into U.S. dollars.

[a]The consumer costs are estimated by multiplying the amount of each commodity that is used for human and industrial consumption (quantities used as livestock feed are excluded) by the difference between its domestic price and import or export price. Generally speaking, no estimates are made of excess consumer costs for fruits and vegetables.

[b]Japanese estimates of excess consumer costs exclude the consumption of rice by the producers of rice. If this consumption is included in the estimates, as is the case for the other estimates, the excess consumer costs are increased by about $2.8 billion in 1979 and $2.5 billion in 1983.

[c]The taxpayer costs for the United States do not include the costs of the food stamp plan or school lunches. These programs are welfare programs and have little or no influence upon farm incomes. If the taxpayer costs were included, it would be necessary to reduce the consumer costs by approximately the same amount since the consumer cost estimates assume that all foods are purchased at the regular market price.

estimates of consumer costs we have compared domestic prices to actual international market prices for the same year. No attempt has been made to reflect what the international prices would have been if there had been minimal protection of agriculture. However, the differences in consumer costs among the various countries should not be seriously affected by using existing international market prices for the analysis. True, the absolute level of consumer costs that we estimate will be too high but this will be true for all countries. Since we have very strictly limited the cost estimates to the price and income support programs, there are numerous governmental costs that we have not included and the exclusions are at least partial offsets to the overestimate of consumer costs that we present.

Table 2 presents a summary of the estimates of consumer and taxpayer costs for Canada, Japan, and the United States. We also compare the total costs to the value of domestic use of agricultural products at world prices for these countries.

We find it difficult to justify these large burdens upon consumers and taxpayers. If we compare these costs to the net income of the farm population from agriculture or the net national income produced by agriculture, it is clear that the costs are very large compared to the net benefits to farm people.

There are those who argue that direct comparison of the taxpayer costs must be made with considerable care. For example, some taxpayer costs have the consequence, even if unintended, of increasing production while other governmental expenditures are used to reduce output and thus to some small degree increase the prices of agricultural products, at least in the short run. But if the basis for evaluating the excess consumer and taxpayer costs is the relationship to farm income, whether the governmental expenditures are used to provide incentives for additional production or are used to induce farmers to reduce the amount produced is irrelevant. While it might be possible to argue that at least some significant part of U.S. governmental expenditures for agriculture, especially in 1982/83, had the effect of reducing U.S. and world agricultural production while expenditures by some other governments increased production of farm products, such an argument in no way makes the approach of one government or the other cost effective in terms of increasing farm incomes.

II. Implications for International Trade

The domestic price and income policies described in Chapter I have effects upon the international trade in farm products. The conflict between price supports and market-oriented trade policy arises whenever the price support is at a level that is actually or potentially above the international market price. For example, assume that a country has a price support for wheat of $200 per ton with the international market price at $150. If there were no barriers to imports, exporters would flood the country with wheat until all of the domestic production were stored and only imported wheat was consumed domestically.[1] The effect of this outcome upon the budgetary costs of the price support program can be easily visualized. The obvious response is to either put a quantitative limit on the amount of wheat that can be imported—an import quota—or to adopt a levy high enough to prevent the cost to local users of any imported wheat being less than $200. The import quota has been the method used by the United States to protect most of its price support programs, especially for wheat, sugar, dairy products, peanuts, and cotton. The levy approach has been used by the European Community while the Japanese have used state-trading, import quotas, and levies to protect domestic price support programs. Since the international market price varies from time to time, the EC adopted the variable levy so that there would be automatic adjustment of the border protection as the difference between the domestic price objective—the threshold price—and the international market price changed.

Programs of price and income support affect the imports and exports of farm products through their influence upon production and con-

---

[1]The example of a price support above the world market price with the consequent effect of almost all domestic output being stored and almost all domestic consumption being that of the imported product is not a hypothetical one. The United States has a price support program for honey and currently the international price for honey is less than the price support level. The duty on honey imports is very low and no additional element of protection at the border has been imposed. As a consequence, in a recent year, almost three-fourths of U.S. honey production was delivered to the government under the price support program and was stored. At the same time, three-fourths of all domestic consumption of honey was imported. The governmental cost was very large compared to the value of the domestically produced honey and it may well be that either the price support for honey will have to be lowered drastically or eliminated or limits will be placed upon the importation of honey. A rather similar outcome has occurred in the European Community for dried raisins where domestically produced raisins were added to stocks and EC consumption consisted mainly of imported raisins.

sumption. If a support measure encourages increased production, imports will decline and, quite possibly, a country may export—usually with subsidies—a product that in the absence of the support program it would import. If the support measure increases consumer prices as well as the return to farmers, consumption will decline. If the product is one that is imported, the consumption decline will decrease imports; if it is one that is exported, exports will be increased solely due to the consumption effects. If the support measure increases both producer and consumer prices, the two effects on trade are additive.

There is a further significant effect of price support measures that utilize variations in international trade to stabilize domestic prices. Domestic price stability is achieved by increasing price instability in international markets. The reason why this is true is quite simple: When domestic prices are stabilized, variations in domestic production due to either weather or farmers' decisions are not reflected in internal prices but instead influence the amount imported or exported. Similarly, variations in domestic demand become reflected in changes in imports or exports since domestic prices do not vary to influence either consumption or production decisions. As will be indicated later, a significant part of international price instability has been estimated to be due to national programs of price stability.

A price support measure that stabilizes prices by varying stocks of farm commodities would not create additional price instability in international markets. In fact, if the stocks are large enough so that variations in world supply and demand can be met by adding to or withdrawing from the stocks, such a policy can act to stabilize international market prices. This was the case during the late 1950s and the 1960s when Canada and the United States held very large stocks of grains and were willing to buy and sell from those stocks within a very narrow price range. The EC has always been a proponent of such a policy in an international sugar agreement.

A. GATT PROVISIONS FOR AGRICULTURE

Before presenting a brief summary of the major effects of the domestic price and income measures upon international trade in each of the areas, we shall summarize the special provisions for agriculture that are included in the General Agreement on Tariffs and Trade (GATT). These permit the maintenance of domestic farm programs that require control of international trade if certain conditions are met—conditions which have not been widely observed.

The title of Article XI is "General Elimination of Quantitative Restrictions." The first paragraph states: "No prohibition or restrictions other than duties, taxes, or other charges, whether made effective by quotas, import or export licenses or other measures, shall be instituted or maintained...." However, Paragraph 2 presents three exceptions to this principle. The first two are of minor significance, but the third permits the use of quantitative import restrictions if one of three conditions are met. This third exception and the attached conditions are stated as follows:

(c) import restrictions on any agricultural or fisheries product, imported in any form, necessary to the enforcement of governmental measures which operate:

(i) to restrict the quantities of the like domestic product permitted to be marketed or produced...; or

(ii) to remove a temporary surplus of the like domestic product...by making the surplus available to certain groups...free of charge or at prices below the current market level; or

(iii) to restrict the quantities permitted to be produced of any animal product the production of which is directly dependent, wholly or mainly, on the imported commodity, if the domestic production of that commodity is relatively negligible.

The GATT provisions with respect to subsidies—Article XVI and the recent Tokyo Round Code—deal with all forms of subsidies that could or do influence the level of exports. Thus it is not only specific export subsidies that are prohibited but any subsidy, such as a deficiency payment, that encourages output expansion. An exception to the general prohibition of subsidies was made for the export of primary, including agricultural, products. The conditions for use of this exception are stated in Section B, Paragraph 3 of Article XVI:

Accordingly, contracting parties should seek to avoid the use of subsidies on the export of primary products. If, however, a contracting party grants directly or indirectly any form of subsidy which operates to increase the export of any primary product from its territory, such subsidy shall not be applied in a manner which results in that contracting party having more than an equitable share of world export trade in that product, account being taken of the shares of the contracting parties in such trade in the product during a previous representative period, and any special factors which may have affected or may be affecting such trade in the product.

The United States was unwilling to have the prohibition against export subsidies apply to agricultural products. This now appears to have been an egregious error on the part of the United States since it is the looseness of Paragraph 3 of Article XVI that has made it possible for contracting parties of GATT to escape international trade disciplines.

Each of the trilateral countries has ignored some of the conditions for the use of import quotas or restrictions with similar effects. Similarly, export subsidies, internal subsidies, deficiency payments and credit subsidies seem not to have been restrained by even the mild exhortation of Article XVI.

B. EFFECTS OF FARM PROGRAMS ON FOREIGN TRADE

It is not our intention to present in detail the possible effects of the farm programs of the trilateral countries upon the volume and value of international trade in agricultural products. Only a brief summary of probable effects seems required since there can be little argument that some of the effects are very large, indeed. We stress often in this report that if all trilateral countries acted in unison to reduce protection for agriculture the adjustments required would be much smaller than if countries acted unilaterally. In other words, how large increases in imports might be or how sharp the decreases in exports might be in each country would depend upon whether the country reduced its trade barriers unilaterally or in concert with all other trilateral countries.

It is true that for some farm products the shifts in trade pattern would be very large. Sugar—heavily protected in all of the trilateral countries—is such a product. The domestic prices of sugar in the United States, the European Community and Japan as of early 1985 are more than five times the international market price. If there were no protection of sugar production in these countries, domestic production of sugar would decline substantially (especially in the United States and Japan, and perhaps rather less in the European Community where there may be some producing areas that could compete with import prices if all of the industrial countries reduced their protection of sugar to some nominal level). There would also be a reduction in the production of sugar from alternative sources, such as corn, with the lower prices that would prevail under market-oriented policies for sugar.

In recent years there have been substantial differences between the domestic prices of dairy products in the trilateral countries and the international market prices. For butter it has not been unusual for domestic prices to be from two to four times the international price;

almost all exports of dry skim milk have involved the use of export subsidies. It is difficult to estimate how large the shifts in the pattern of trade would be if protection were significantly reduced in the industrial countries. It is clear, however, that the international market price for dairy products would increase significantly—even with rather small increases in dairy imports in the United States, Canada, and Japan and some reduction in exports from the European Community. The milk output for New Zealand and Australia combined—the primary non-trilateral suppliers—is only 13 million tons compared to about 170 million tons in North America, Japan, and the European Community. Lower domestic prices would also result in somewhat higher consumption.

Rather belatedly both the United States and the European Community have taken steps to reduce milk production. In the United States the program involves payments to farmers for reducing their dairy herds and reductions in the support price for milk if government purchases continue at significant levels. In the European Community individual farm quotas have been established and farmers are penalized at a high rate if they exceed their quotas. During their first years, both programs have had some success in reducing milk production. But it has to be said that neither policy is designed to make the dairy sector more market-oriented. In both cases, the primary cause of the policy shift was the need to reduce governmental costs. In the United States it appears that the objective is that of moving from surplus milk production to self-sufficiency; when self-sufficiency is reached the pressure for further adjustment in milk production will dissipate. The new milk program of the European Community has a great deal in common with the Canadian milk programs of the past decades. In Canada farmers have been assigned individual quotas for producing either industrial milk or milk for fluid use. These programs have limited milk production to approximately the level of Canadian consumption.

This is an appropriate place to note the major trade effects of exchange rate changes alongside farm policies. As of early 1985 there is only modest protection of wheat production in the European Community. With the sharp rise in the foreign exchange value of the dollar, the Community prices of wheat are now very close to the international market level. This is not yet true for maize and barley, but even there the margins of protection are currently much below what they were a few years ago. The rapid growth of U.S. grain exports during the 1970s was made possible, at least in part, by the substantial decline in the foreign exchange value of the dollar.

The protection provided grain production in the United States, Japan, and the European Community has reduced the opportunities of others for exporting grains. Aside from the farm programs of importers of grain damaging exporters, the farm programs of exporters can themselves have adverse effects on their own exports. The decline in U.S. exports of grain in recent years has been due to the combined effects of the sharp rise in the foreign exchange value of the dollar and the rigid price support or loan rates for grain (and supply management programs reducing grain production in most years since 1977). A group of Australian agricultural economists concluded that if the United States moved to a market-oriented grain policy by lowering price supports and abolishing output restraints "its grain export sector would regain some of the competitiveness that it achieved in the 1970s but has lost recently....If there is a move to market-related support prices in the USA, international grain prices are likely to be lower than would be the case if the current U.S. policies remained essentially unchanged."[2] Except for large subsidies for the transportation of grain from producing areas to the ports for export, Canada does not have programs that materially subsidize grain production.

The world beef and veal market has changed radically over the past quarter century, due largely to domestic farm programs. In the past, beef exports came primarily from Latin America, New Zealand and Australia. In some recent years, aided by significant supports and export subsidies, the European Community has been the world's largest exporter of beef. In 1964 the United States enacted legislation permitting import quotas on beef and veal, subsequently negotiating so-called voluntary export restraints to achieve the purpose intended for the import quotas. In spite of the restraints, the United States is now the world's largest importer of beef. Japan provides a high degree of protection for beef and controls imports through the use of import quotas.

Aside from the effects of farm programs on the volume of international trade, a number of studies have been undertaken by research organizations and at universities on how much effect these interventions have upon the level and variability of world market prices. (Effects on farm income, land prices, capital gains and losses, and the influence of exchange rates have not been analyzed by these studies.) The results of some of these studies are summarized in Section E of the Appendix. It should be noted that in these studies the drastic changes

---

[2] J. Longmire, P. Perkins and W.T. Coyle, "Developments in U.S. Grain Policies: Looking Towards the 1985 Farm Bill," *Quarterly Review of Rural Economy* (1984), p. 254.

of the exchange rates have not been taken into account, since such studies refer to conditions of the late 1970s prior to the recent sharp adjustments in exchange rates.

As for the level of prices, the general conclusion is that for most of the considered products (dairy and sugar were not taken into account) the international market prices that prevail with existing degrees of protection depart rather little from the projected prices under trade liberalization. For instance, international market prices for grain may have been depressed by 10 to 15 percent in recent years. However, whatever the extent of price distortion in international market prices due to current levels of protection, the adjustments required as a result of market-oriented policies will be significantly less than appears when one compares current domestic and international market prices. In saying this, it is assumed, as we strongly recommend, that the trilateral countries act in unison in moving to market-oriented policies.

As for price variability, the much greater variability under current policies than under the assumption of free trade results from the nature of agricultural protection that prevails in many countries. Agricultural protection *per se*, as noted above, need not result in increasing price variability in international markets (and thus in the countries where international prices are directly reflected in domestic prices). It is the form of protection that causes the increased variability. Protection of agriculture that functions by stabilizing domestic prices exclusively through varying imports and exports of commodities destabilizes international market prices. It does so through using import and export volume changes to meet any variation in domestic supply and demand, preventing internal price changes from absorbing at least part of the variability (for estimates of possible effects, see Appendix).

C. EFFECTS ON DEVELOPING COUNTRY EXPORTS

Our discussion indicates that the domestic agricultural policies of the trilateral countries have reduced the opportunities for efficient producers to export their products. It is rather less serious when the loss of opportunities affects only the high income industrial economies than when developing countries are prevented from taking full advantage of their comparative advantages in agriculture. A legitimate though generally ignored concern in judging our domestic farm policies is how much the policies restrict profitable agricultural exports from the developing countries. It is difficult to measure this impact with any exactitude. However, the economists who have addressed the question agree that the effects have been significant and that the export markets of the developing countries have been adversely affected. In the cases of sugar and of grains in the 1960s the effects have been substantial.

A detailed and systematic analysis was undertaken at the International Food Policy Research Institute, based on the market conditions of the late 1970s. This study asked what increases in exports by the developing countries would occur if the industrial countries reduced their protection of agriculture by 50 percent for 99 agricultural products.[3] Thus the assumption was not that of free trade, but only that the difference between domestic and international market prices would be reduced by half. The 56 developing countries included in the study were projected to gain an increase in the value of agricultural exports of $3.4 billion in 1977 prices. The increase represented 12.4 percent of the value of LDC exports of agricultural products in 1975-77. Almost a third of the increased LDC agricultural exports were projected to result from lower levels of protection for sugar. The developing countries would realize both larger export volume and higher prices.

[3]Alberto Valdes and Joachim Zietz, *Agricultural Protection in OECD Countries: Its Cost to Less-Developed Countries*, Research Report 21 of the International Food Policy Research Institute (Washington, D.C.: December 1980).

III. Moving to More Market-Oriented Policies

A. TRANSITIONAL ADJUSTMENTS

Governments and the interests that they serve and represent resist the types of changes required to move from interventionist programs to market-oriented programs. This is true not only with respect to agriculture, but is a difficult political and economic problem whenever an industry or sector is protected through market interventions and trade restrictions. The costs of removing the protective measures are relatively easy to see (even if difficult to calculate), while the benefits of the changes are much more diffused throughout the economy.

The transition costs are of three main kinds, namely loss of current farm income, adjustment to alternative employment, and loss in value of assets (both on farms and in agribusiness). We believe that these are real problems and that, for both political and economic reasons, time and assistance would be required to make the transition as painless as possible.

This is perhaps the appropriate point to note that, when we speak of lowering the levels of protection and moving to market-oriented farm policies, we are not advocating that levels of protection everywhere be zero. Our position is that over time the levels of protection should be significantly reduced and domestic producers faced with some degree of competition from the international markets. Thus if production could remain profitable with a moderate level of protection there is no strong reason why protection of this magnitude should not be provided.

Making domestic farm programs more market-oriented would require significant adjustments in agriculture in each of the trilateral countries. It is not obvious how severe these adjustments would be in some cases—especially dairy products and sugar—because current world market prices are seriously distorted. The distortions for other important traded products are relatively small according to the available evidence, namely 10 percent or so compared to what the free trade prices would be.

In the United States the most significant resource adjustments would be required for dairy, sugar, and peanuts. Part of the adjustment process is already underway in dairy, though only to the extent required to reduce governmental costs of the price support program. The effect of the current adjustment process upon international trade will be very small since most of the excess supplies of milk have been absorbed domestically. However, achieving self-sufficiency in milk production does not address the question of how competitive the U.S. dairy industry is. It seems highly probable that under a market-oriented trade regime the United States would import a significant percentage of its dairy products. How large that percentage would be depends upon the level of international prices of dairy products if there were greater market-orientation in national dairy programs. Since the U.S. market for dairy products is so large compared to output in the low cost dairy producing countries (primarily New Zealand and Australia), if the United States imported as little as 10 percent of its domestic use the effect upon international dairy prices would be substantial.

Under a market-oriented trade regime sugar production in the United States would decline to low levels and might eventually be abandoned. While the losses in capital values would be substantial, the savings to consumers in very few years would be greater than the capital losses to sugar producers and refiners. There would also be a reduction in the production of high fructose sugar from corn and, in turn, in corn gluten meal. The profitability of high fructose sugar has been substantially enhanced by the high price supports for sugar since 1981.

There are two grains that would be less profitable if the farm price support, target price, and supply management programs were eliminated. These are wheat and rice. The producers of each of these crops have received substantial payments as supplements to their market returns. But much of the adjustment would probably come through lower land values and only to a modest degree through output reduction.

In Canada the farm sectors that would need to adjust are dairy and wheat and barley. There would be significant capital losses if the output quotas for milk, poultry and eggs were eliminated. Milk output would decline, perhaps by five to ten percent. There seems no reason why poultry and egg production should not be competitive in world markets. The adjustments for wheat and barley would be minor, perhaps no more than two or three years of output growth.

In Japan the major adjustment problems would be for grain (including rice) producers. Grain products have been protected to a much greater degree than have poultry, eggs, pork, vegetables and fruits other than oranges. Producer prices of grain in Japan exceed world market levels by a factor of four or more. While it is true that current levels of rice prices are higher than would be required for rice self-sufficiency in Japan, it has to be recognized that low levels of protection for grain products would impose very large adjustment costs upon Japanese farmers. While there are clear opportunities for reducing the costs of producing rice through farm enlargement, similar possibilities probably do not exist for wheat and barley.

A market-oriented policy with moderate levels of protection would require significant adjustments for Japanese dairy and beef producers. As we have argued, the current international prices for dairy products are seriously distorted by trade interventions. If these prices increased significantly—and a doubling for butter and dry skim milk is not out of the question—the adjustment problems for the dairy sector in Japan might well be manageable. Since beef prices are not significantly depressed in international markets, the fed-beef producers would be faced with the need to adjust. However, a large fraction of the beef production in Japan is a byproduct of the dairy sector and depends upon the production of milk. Orange production might well be profitable with moderate levels of protection.

In the case of the European Community, a reduction in support to the agricultural sector would largely mean reduced prices. Although there is strong evidence of a positive supply response to higher prices, there is only weaker evidence of a negative supply response to lower prices. Real prices received by producers have fallen since the mid-1970s for many commodities, but production has continued to rise—which may be explained by the strong influence of technological developments and structural change, together with profit-enhancing policies that reduce farmers' costs but are not reflected in output prices. The historical experience may indicate that prices would have to fall substantially to reduce output (in the absence of other output restricting measures, such as quotas), in order to compensate for the inherent technological and structural production-increasing factors.

It is too early to judge the effects of the adjustments as a result of the recent quota arrangements for milk in Europe, which aim at a five percent reduction in European production in the next five years.

In the case of sugar, the quotas and producer levies have resulted in some decrease in the area producing sugar beet since 1982 and in sugar beet production. The successful implementation of the quota schemes will quickly reduce the quantities available for export and ease the downward pressure on world prices. However, their successful implementation depends on the levels at which the quota is fixed, the prices guaranteed to producers and the effectiveness of penalties in the cases of production in excess of quota. In the long run, the inflexibility of quota arrangements may not contribute to facilitating agricultural adjustment and may therefore give cause for concern, particularly in view of the still untapped potential for increasing output.

In the case of cereals, where no quota policies are envisaged in Europe, a policy of more market-oriented prices would probably result in strengthening the acceptability of the Community as an exporter, in increased internal consumption of feed grains, and in stabilization in the use of substitutes. As the prospects of technological advance, notably in wheat, are promising, real prices would have to fall to reduce production. To absorb further potential exports, alternative profitable outlets for industrial and other purposes (e.g., alcohol) should be sought.

In all of our countries, for both political and economic reasons, time and assistance would be required to make the transition to the economic environment of a more market-oriented trade regime as painless as possible for the sectors that would have to adjust by transferring resources to other uses.

While there may be some agreement that a period of five years would be approximately the appropriate length of time for adjustment to be largely completed, there may be need for different approaches during the transition period in different situations. Where the degree of adjustment required is relatively modest, as is the case with wheat in North America, a specified gradual elimination of current subsidies might be the appropriate response. However, where the resource adjustments or the capital losses would be large, more extensive actions may be desirable.

Where there would be substantial capital losses through the elimination of the value of output quotas, it would be in the clear economic interest of consumers to have the government pay for part of the value of the quotas if this were the only way to eliminate the quotas and the higher prices. The savings in lower consumer prices would soon more than cover the payments for the quotas, even if the full value of the quotas were purchased by the government. Several research projects have estimated that the market value of the quotas in North America for dairy and poultry products and tobacco are based on a discount rate of 25 percent. In other words, the farmers who purchase the quotas know that there is a substantial risk that the programs that give value to the quotas may be modified, even eliminated. Consequently, the present values of the quotas are a little less than four years of the anticipated benefits.

B. MARKET-ORIENTED POLICIES
AND FARM INCOMES OVER TIME

The preceding section focuses on the costs that must be borne by any transition, even an extended one, from current interventionist policies to more market-oriented policies. Three transition costs were noted above—short-run declines in farm incomes, the loss in asset values from lower market prices, and the costs of adjusting to other employment.

We turn now to the longer-run effects of market-oriented policies upon the incomes of farm people. Our position on the effect of farm price supports upon the level and distribution of incomes among farm families has been well stated in a recent OECD publication:

> Income support through prices normally results in a higher income for the "national farm" than in the absence of such measures, thereby improving the income situation in agriculture as a whole compared to that in other sectors. On the other hand, some resources will remain in agriculture which would otherwise have shifted elsewhere. When a system of general non-selective price support is in operation the larger farmers benefit more than the smaller ones who are most in need of income support. Further, larger producers benefit more from a rise in support prices (about in proportion to each farmer's sales) than their smaller counterparts. Thus disparities within agriculture tend to increase.

> Price supports affect incomes of owner-occupiers and tenant farmers in different ways. Higher returns to farmers due to price supports will result in rising land prices and, after a time lag which may be rather long in countries where rents are controlled, in higher rents. The owner-occupier who retains the whole extra income and benefits from capital gains on the land finds himself in a stronger position when he wishes to finance farm modernisation or expansion programmes. The tenant who pays a higher rent may find his landlord reluctant to invest in the farm and may be unable to finance necessary farm improvements.[1]

The difference in the effects of price supports on the incomes of farm owners and tenants is important. It may be noted, in addition, that when new farmers enter agriculture they are forced to purchase their land at the higher prices resulting from the price supports. Consequently the benefits that go to land owners go to existing land owners and not to those who will purchase their land after the price

---

[1] *The Implications of Different Means of Agricultural Income Support* (Paris: OECD, 1983), pp. 43-44.

support or subsidy programs were established. One of the reasons that it is so difficult to move from interventionist to market-oriented policies is that many current farmers have actually paid the higher prices for land or have purchased quotas or the rights to produce. The current farmers understandably are reluctant to suffer the capital loss for an asset which they purchased in the expectation that current policies would remain unchanged.

The level of farm prices determines only to some degree how many people will be engaged in agriculture. One of the major factors is the labor market, as was observed by Dale Hathaway, one of the most respected U.S. agricultural economists and former Under Secretary of Agriculture:

> More than other markets in our economy, the labor market acts to determine who goes into farming—and when and whether to leave it. During most of the period of the 1940s through the 1960s, the labor market was crucial in determining farm income per person. This came about because such a major imbalance existed between the number of people dependent upon agriculture and the number who could make a decent living there assuming any likely range of farm commodity prices and capital costs.
>
> In the years before World War II, per capita incomes of farm people were well under 50 percent of the per capita incomes received by non-farm people. In some years of the 1930s, the average farm person received from all sources an amount of income no more than one-third that received by his non-farm cousin. And chances are the non-farm cousin wasn't doing too well either.
>
> During the war, the differential began to narrow. In the last half of the 1940s, per capita income of farm people averaged 60 percent of the per capita income of non-farm people from all sources.
>
> In the 1950s, however, farm income per person again fell behind—remaining mostly static while the per capita income of non-farm people rose by more than a third. In the last half of the 1950s, the per capita income of farm people was only one-half the per capita income received by people living off the farm.
>
> In the early 1960s, we could see the beginning of adjustment. By the end of the decade, per capita income on farms averaged above $2,000 compared with around $3,000 for non-farm people. For the 5 years 1965 through 1969 people living on farms averaged 71 percent of the per capita income of people living off the farm.
>
> In more recent years, this percentage has risen to 85 or more—although this of course varies from year to year.

So—the labor market did adjust. But the adjustments were difficult for many. Despite government efforts to deal with these
difficulties, it appears in retrospect that no government policy or
program was significant in aiding the adjustment or softening the
pain of adjustment for farm people.

The quote is from a speech made while he was still a major official of the
U.S. Department of Agriculture during the Carter Administration.

The substantial reduction in the income differences among U.S.
farm families on farms of different sizes, as measured by value of sales,
is worthy of note. In 1960 the farm families on the two-fifths of the
farms with the lowest value of sales had incomes from all sources equal
to 27 percent of the income of the 7.5 percent of the farms with the
largest sales. In 1980 the income of families on the smallest farms, again
from all sources, was 47 percent of the income of the families of the
largest farms. The largest 7.5 percent of the farms had net assets of
almost two million dollars, more than ten times the net assets of the
smallest 40 percent of the farms as measured by sales. This improvement in the relative income position of the families on small farms was
due primarily to the increase in income from non-farm sources. It may
be noted that the average incomes of the farm families on the smaller
farms has increased relative to the national mean income for all families—from 57 percent in 1960 to 75 percent in 1970 and to 92 percent in
1980. As Dale Hathaway noted, these improvements in farm incomes
were not due to governmental agricultural policies but to the alternative possibilities in the labor market.

In Canada approximately half of the farms may be classified as full-
time farms, if full-time farms are defined as farms operated by families
that have net farm income greater than off-farm income. Even the
farms classified as full-time receive approximately a quarter of their
family incomes from off-farm sources. For all Canadians living on
farms, nearly three fourths of their income was from off-farm sources
in 1980.

Table 3 presents income data for all Canadian families and for farm
families classified in four different ways. The classifications are not
exclusive—a given family could be included in all four categories. But
the data are relevant to the present discussion. First, over time farm
family incomes have increased relative to the average level for all
families. Second, there is very little difference in the farm income levels
by the degree of importance of farm income to total income. A clear
implication of this is that farm families living on farms that would
provide a low total return for their labor, capital and management have
adjusted by increasing their off-farm incomes to achieve rough equality

TABLE 3

**Average Net Income from All Sources of Farm Families
Compared with that of All Families, Canada, 1965, 1971, 1976 and 1981**
(Canadian dollars)

		FARM FAMILIES			
	ALL FAMILIES	WITH ONE MEMBER WHO REPORTED SOME NET FARM INCOME	WHO LIVE ON CENSUS FARMS	WITH ONE MEMBER WHO REPORTS FARMING AS PRINCIPAL OCCUPATION	WITH ONE MEMBER WHO REPORTS NET FARM INCOME AS MAJOR SOURCE OF INCOME
1965	5,779	4,302	4,209	4,301	4,134
1971	8,845	7,313	6,604	6,533	6,398
1976	16,095	18,018	15,862	16,767	16,160
1981	25,641	29,335	26,032	26,519	27,808

Source: Data for 1965, 1971 and 1976 from G. L. Brinkman, *Farm Incomes in Canada* (Ottawa:
Supply and Services, 1981), Table 3.5; 1981 data provided by Monique Berutty,
Statistics Canada.

TABLE 4

**Per-capita Household Expenditures in Japan:
Comparison between Farm Households and Wage-earning Households**
(wage-earning households = 100)

			NATIONWIDE	CITIES, TOWNS AND VILLAGES WITH A POPULATION LESS THAN 50,000	TOWNS AND VILLAGES ONLY
Average all farm households		FY1970	95.3	103.5	103.4
		FY1975	107.1	109.1	108.1
		FY1980	113.4	119.4	119.7
		FY1981	111.4	116.7	117.6
		FY1982	110.6	112.8	111.9
FY1982	Full-time farm households (with a core male full-time farmer)		88.8	90.6	89.9
	Class I part-time farm households (with a temporary wage earner)		91.8	93.7	92.9
	Class II part-time farm households (with a permanent wage earner)		116.2	118.6	117.7

Source: Ministry of Agriculture, Forestry and Fisheries, *The State of Japan's Agriculture
1983, A Summary Report* (Tokyo: April 1984).

with the farm families living on farms of sufficient size to provide all or most of their incomes. The data indicate that the substantial income transfers that farm programs provide have not resulted in higher incomes for the farm families who receive most of them than for other farm families who receive little or nothing from the farm programs.

Japanese farm families now receive about three fourths of their incomes from non-farm sources. To a remarkable degree, in spite of the enormous differences in agricultural resources and farm policies, the income patterns in Japan, the United States and Canada are very similar. This is true in terms of the income levels of farm families relative to non-farm families and the approximate equality of farm family incomes with varying degrees of importance of farm income in total income. Table 4 compares the incomes of farm families and "wage-earning households" in Japan and also compares incomes among farm families in terms of the dependence upon farm incomes. The incomes of full-time farm families compare reasonably favorably with the incomes of all farm families (about 80%) and wage-earning households (about 90%), but that is all that has been achieved by the very high farm prices for all grains and certain other products, such as beef.

While there are less data on the importance of non-farm income to farm families and on the income levels of farm families with different degrees of dependence upon agriculture for the EC, the Commission of the European Communities in its 1983 report on *The Agricultural Situation in the Community* noted that in 1977 only 37 percent of the farm holders in the EC-9 (i.e., without Greece, Spain, and Portugal) found full-time employment on their farms and that only 55 percent of farm holders work for more than 50 percent of their time on their farms.

The report clearly recognizes the importance of the general economic situation which confronts farm families as a critical element in determining farm family incomes.

> ...the importance of a second income to those working in agriculture—in 1975 it was found that about one quarter of farm holders had a second gainful activity. In this context, it should be borne in mind that the availability of a second gainful activity to part-time holders varies significantly from region to region—for example, while the majority of part-time farm holders in Southern Germany have a second income earned outside their farm, in the Mezzogiorno (southern Italy) few such opportunities exist and most farm holders are under-employed.

This quotation is fully consistent with earlier reports of the Commission that the Common Agricultural Policy had not been as effective as anticipated in reducing quite substantial regional differences in farm incomes within the EC. High farm prices appear not to have been especially effective in reducing income inequality either within regions or between regions. The 1980 report on *The Agricultural Situation in the Community* spoke to the issue as follows:

> During the period from 1964/65 to 1976/77, regional disparities in agricultural incomes (as measured by gross value-added per agricultural worker) increased in the Community. The ratio between the regions with the highest agricultural incomes and those with the lowest rose from 5:1 to 6:1.

> Generally speaking, the regions with above-average levels of agricultural income are to be found in a favourable general economic context; the converse is true of regions with a low level of agricultural income.

C. DIMINISHING AGRICULTURAL EMPLOYMENT IN GROWING ECONOMIES

The process of economic growth everywhere requires that after a time the absolute level of employment in agriculture must decline. No country has been able to avoid the decline in farm employment. Available evidence appears to indicate that the rate of decline in percentages in farm employment since the mid-1950s is quite independent of differences in the level of farm prices. Farm employment must decline because of the low income elasticities of demand for farm products and because productivity change in agriculture in the industrial countries has been at least as rapid as in the rest of the economy. Increases in labor productivity in agriculture have generally been greater than in industrial employment, in part because of the substitution of capital for labor which seems to be a part of the process of modernizing agriculture.

Could the reduction in farm employment be slowed down by maintaining relatively high product prices? The answer to this question seems to be: not by very much. It is highly likely, of course, that if farm prices were permanently raised by 10 percent, employment in agriculture would be increased for a period of time. But as soon as earnings in agriculture and the rest of the economy returned to their usual relationships, farm employment would decline each year at approximately the same rate as before the increase in farm prices. An increase in farm prices of 10 percent would have an effect upon farm labor earnings equal to no more than three or four years of growth in real wages. Thus the increase in farm labor earnings associated with the increase in farm prices would rather quickly be offset by the increase in alternative earnings in the non-farm sector and farm people, as always, would need to seek other and more rewarding uses of their time.

If one compares the level of farm prices across countries with the annual rates of decline in farm employment, one finds no significant relationship (see Tables F-1 and F-2 in Section F of the Appendix). High farm prices are not associated with low rates of decline and relatively low farm prices are not associated with high rates of decline in farm employment. A comparison of Japan and Canada illustrates this very well. During the 1960s farm employment in Japan declined by four percent annually compared to just 2.7 percent in Canada (Table F-2). Or compare Germany and the United States. In each segment of time from 1955 through 1979 (1955-60, 1960-70 and 1970-79) the rate of decline of farm employment in Germany was either the same as or greater than in the United States (Table F-2). Nor can one tell when Ireland entered the Common Market from the data on the annual decline in farm employment.

Under conditions of economic growth, if farm people are to share in the benefits of economic growth, real agricultural labor earnings must increase over time at the same rate as nonagricultural wages. (Real agricultural labor earnings as used here includes the returns to the management and labor input of farm operators and unpaid family workers as well as payments to hired farm workers.) If there are few barriers to labor mobility, farm labor earnings will increase at approximately the same rate as non-farm labor earnings. In fact, during the past three decades the barriers to mobility in the industrial countries have declined. Put another way, in recent decades the costs of mobility have fallen and, as a result, the differentials in earnings between farm and non-farm people have declined. The reduction in costs of mobility *inter alia* have been due to reductions in the real costs of transportation and of acquiring information. The general availability of the automobile or the bus plus the improvement and extension of roads has sharply reduced the costs of both moving and commuting. Further, the costs of information have been sharply reduced through the nearly universal availability of radio, television and the telephone as well as the printed media. The reduction in the income differentials between the countryside and the city, due to reduction in costs of either moving or commuting, has been an added element in reducing farm employment.

Due to the substantial adjustments that farm people must make to the changing conditions in a growing economy, governments should have rural development policies that help to ensure non-farm employment opportunities. The more development there is of non-farm activities in rural areas, the less difficult will be the transition from farm to non-farm employment. In particular, the viability of part-time farming depends upon the availability of non-farm jobs in or near rural communities.

There is a clear need for governments to recognize that the influence of agricultural policy upon the incomes and well-being of farm people has declined over the years and will continue to decline in the years ahead. This is due, in large part, to the effective integration of agriculture and farm people into the economies of the trilateral countries. On the other hand, in a situation of a stagnant economy with continuing technological progress in agriculture, remaining structural deficiencies and regional isolation, lack of mobility and alternative employment possibilities, and the need for environmental balance, agricultural policies can play an important role for the development (i.e., incomes) of the rural population.

The amount of income that farm people must obtain from non-farm sources has increased and will continue to increase. Consequently it is essential that, as agricultural programs designed to assist farm people evolve in the years ahead, there be emphasis upon rural development policies as well as upon market and price policies.

We want to make it clear that in advocating more market-oriented agricultural policies we are not arguing for dismantling the many socio-structural measures that benefit disadvantaged farmers. These measures have almost no effect upon agricultural production and trade. Some of the measures, such as social security, simply bring farmers within systems that operate in the rest of the economy. Certain of the structural measures maintain a level of rural economic activity and employment but affect only a very small share of agricultural production. In a few cases, some measures are specifically designed to help farmers cease their farming activities.

Nor do we suggest that agricultural research and extension should be minimized. The benefits of general policies that improve production efficiency are widely distributed among the citizens of our countries. Agricultural research results benefit farmers no more than any other individual since such research acts to lower the cost of producing food and thus primarily serves the interests of consumers. Some might argue that the more agricultural research contributes to increased productivity in farming, the more difficult are the adjustment problems that must be surmounted by farmers. There is validity in this position, but the alternative of living with a static and gradually less productive agriculture is even less attractive.

IV. RECOMMENDATIONS

The adjustment of domestic farm programs is an important but extremely difficult task. It appears that the next two or three years offer the best opportunity for progress of any period since World War II. The internal costs of current farm programs in the trilateral countries—costs to both taxpayers and consumers—have become more politically salient; and the external costs—in terms of tensions among the trilateral countries and with other OECD countries and the developing countries—have risen in the market conditions of the 1980s.

It is quite clear what is required if domestic farm policy regimes are to contribute to an improved international situation for all producers and consumers. First, domestic programs must be made more market-oriented. This means that the signals and incentives provided to farmers must more fully reflect actual market conditions rather than some inflexible formula or political process with little or no connection to underlying supply and demand conditions. We are not advocating that levels of protection everywhere be zero. Our position is that over time the levels of protection should be significantly reduced and domestic producers faced with some degree of competition from the international markets. We are heartened by some recent modifications of price guarantees and loan rates that do more adequately reflect market conditions.[1]

Second, the trilateral countries should move together in achieving more market-oriented policies for agriculture. Although there are good economic arguments for greater market orientation even with other countries standing still, the chances of significantly reducing the degree of protection provided agriculture are far better with all trilateral areas moving together. The fear that lowering protection unilaterally would result in a flood of imports with little or no prospect of offsetting advantages in international markets makes greater market orientation most unlikely unless carried out in concert with other major importers and exporters of farm products.

Third, it must be recognized that it is not possible to move to market-oriented policies all at once. It is essential that farm people be given a

---

[1]Some of those we consulted stressed the need to give attention to the effects of agricultural development on the environmental balance. We share this concern. The move to more market-oriented policies need not make this any harder to achieve.

transition period within which to adjust to the new policy framework. Since the extent of the required adjustment differs from commodity to commodity and country to country, it is not possible to specify across the board how long transition periods should be. But as a general guideline, a period of five to seven years should be adequate for most of the necessary adjustments.

Finally, during the transition period there should be no additional trade barriers introduced nor should existing barriers be unilaterally broadened. This condition is extremely important since farm people must be given confidence that the adjustments that they are making will not be offset or their effectiveness reduced by new or broadened trade restrictions adopted by other countries. Similarly, there should not be new implicit or explicit export subsidies.

In the pages to follow we turn first to priority adjustments for the United States, Canada, the European Community, and Japan. Naturally enough, the most important adjustments differ from country to country. As we have stressed repeatedly, however, it is important that the trilateral countries move together—and the final part of this chapter turns to agricultural negotiations in a new GATT Round, which we very much support. Much of the negotiation will focus on strengthening GATT rules—on import restrictions and export subsidies. The middle section of this chapter addresses current famine conditions in Africa and food aid.

A. PRIORITY ADJUSTMENTS

The United States

The objective of U.S. farm policy should be to eliminate over the next five years nearly all protection for farm products, both those competing with imports and those exported into international markets. There are significant problems in moving from the present programs to the desired policy position. The most pressing problem as this is written is the debt situation that confronts a significant fraction of the 650,000 farms that account for 87 percent of all U.S. farm sales. With declining land prices, continuing high interest rates, and net farm incomes at much lower levels than several years ago, many of these farmers will be forced to liquidate their operations unless some significant financial relief is forthcoming or the level of farm incomes increases substantially within the next year or two. This debt situation clearly must be given consideration during the transition period, but without losing sight of adjustment objectives.

a. Price supports and commodity loan rates should be continued as a part of market-oriented policies, but the primary purpose of price supports should be to assist farmers in orderly marketing, not to inflate market prices or to affect the distribution of farm products between domestic and foreign markets. Farm price supports set at 85 percent of the average market prices of the three preceding years would be consistent with these objectives.

b. Deficiency payments for grains and cotton need to be gradually eliminated. These direct payments from the government are paid to farmers per unit of output when market prices fall below specified "target prices"—prices higher than those the government stands ready to support in the marketplace. These payments encourage increased and unwanted production of farm products; and are also a form of export subsidy.

c. Dairy price supports should be reduced to a level that would eliminate domestic production in excess of domestic consumption and then further reduced to determine if U.S. dairy producers could compete with unsubsidized dairy exports from other producing areas. The quantitative import restrictions on dairy products should be gradually relaxed and dairy product imports should be subject only to the prevailing tariff duties.

d. The beef import control law should be rather quickly liberalized and then abolished. This law has little effect upon beef imports or domestic prices, yet it is a disruptive factor in smooth international relations.

e. Federal income tax provisions that encourage investment in agriculture should be eliminated. Some provisions, commonly known as tax shelters, are of little direct benefit to full-time farmers. In many cases, it is necessary to have significant non-farm income in order to take advantage of the tax shelters. Thus these shelters encourage non-farmers to make uneconomic investments in agriculture. Other tax provisions, such as capital gains treatment for breeding herds and fast depreciation for machinery and equipment, also have the effect of encouraging investment and increasing productive capacity.

Canada
a. The most obvious and important commodity area in which Canada could make concessions to its trading partners by changing its internal policies and accompanying trade arrangements is milk. There are no compelling strategic or food security reasons why Canada should be 100 percent self-sufficient in fluid milk and butter, and nearly so in

cheese. And the pursuit of this objective involves socially regressive and economically wasteful ongoing income transfers to dairy farmers from Canadian consumers and taxpayers, requires that Canada impairs the legitimate trade interests of efficient foreign suppliers, and results in her dumping large quantities of product on world markets. Technically, this change in policy could be accomplished by lowering the quantity of industrial milk supported under the formula pricing/supply management program. The willingness of others, notably the European Community, to engage in parallel liberalization would be crucial in accomplishing this adjustment in Canada.

b. The international competitiveness of Canadian grains and oilseeds has been directly enhanced by the large transport subsidy on the movement of these commodities from the Prairies to export positions and the funding from the public purse of investments in railway modernization. The federal government has taken the first step in capping this "Crow Gap" subsidy—in 1983 legislation limiting the annual subsidy to $659 million (the 1981/82 level) plus a falling share of subsequent freight cost increases. Further steps to reduce this subsidy should be taken over time, particularly in a context of multilateral liberalization. The subsidy should be paid to producers, not to the railways.

c. Provincial "top-loading" of federal price and income stabilization programs should be phased out, particularly where they go beyond stabilization and become a permanent subsidy. The price and margin stabilization programs of the Canadian federal government (with some exceptions) have been more market-oriented than those of any other trilateral government—providing a market-determined, low-slung safety net in low price periods rather than guarantees of remunerative prices and returns. These federal programs, however, have been supplemented over time by a variety of provincial supports.

d. Pricing and quota arrangements for eggs and poultry meat should be changed. Since these arrangements are in conformity with GATT, foreign suppliers cannot complain loudly; but the domestic costs are substantial. The 5,000 registered producers of eggs and poultry have been permitted to use their monopoly powers to transfer to themselves around $100 million a year from Canadian consumers and to pump up the aggregate value of their quota rights to well over $1 billion.

The European Community
a. The CAP has a quite rigid and high price system of guarantees for cereals, protected by levies on imports and subsidies on exports. At the same time there is a complete free trade system for competing pro-

teins, fats and oils, and grain substitutes. In order to install a more market-oriented system, the Community should change towards a more flexible guarantee system for cereals that is aligned to the prices of its main competitors. In return for this major change in the Community's cereal price regime, the United States should be willing, in the context of trade negotiations, to allow the Community over time to bring the internal market price level of proteins, oils and fats, and other substitutes in line with cereal prices in the new cereal price regime. The adjustment in Community cereal prices will itself, of course, reduce the price advantage of cereal substitutes. The alignment of Community cereal prices with "prices of main competitors" would incorporate in Community prices the add-on to market prices represented by deficiency payments to producers in some competing countries.

b. The Community in 1984 established a quota system for milk—developed as a five-year arrangement—in order to bring down the surpluses of dairy products. This regime is expected to diminish production by about five percent and stabilize it until 1989. To prevent this system becoming a permanent impediment for economic production of milk, the Community should develop in time an alternative pricing system that itself keeps production in line with market demand without the use of quotas.

c. The beef guarantee system—and its price level—should be modified in order to orient producers more to the market and give less incentive to sell beef to the Community Intervention Agencies.

d. In order to prevent more market-oriented policies being frustrated by all kinds of distorting national subsidies, the Community should effectively operate a rigid set of rules to assure fair competition within the Community.

Japan

As mentioned in Chapter I, from 1980 Japanese agricultural policy has swung toward increasing productivity. If the following adjustments of Japanese agricultural policy are part of a joint effort of all trilateral countries, the modest swing toward greater market orientation can be powerfully reinforced.

a. "Food security" should be reformulated. Although we are sympathetic to the strong Japanese concern with food security, the present method of seeking food security involves exceedingly high costs. "Food security" should not be an excuse for failing to pursue efforts to reduce the costs to consumers and taxpayers of assuring Japan's food supply. Even without importing a single ton of rice, the rice price in Japan could be far lower than it is now if the present production quota system to avoid rice surpluses is modified. As for non-rice grains, a stockpiling program would be much more cost effective than the present wheat-barley program in supporting food security. Food security should be seen in terms of the assured availability of supplies not self-sufficiency in production. The above changes will make the Japanese food security program more market-oriented.

b. Rice price support should be lowered. There is no doubt that the real core of efforts to modify Japanese agricultural support policy lies in the possibility of productivity increases in rice production, which occupies half of Japanese arable land. The majority of rice growers—which in general cultivate less than one hectare—depend on their non-farm activities for their major source of income. Moreover, significant numbers of these part-time rice growers do not have any young successor in line to take over their farms. There is an enormous untapped potential for increasing productivity of rice production in Japan, particularly through farm enlargement. As stated above, the present quota system has to be re-examined. The structural improvement program will be more cost effective if the program is accompanied by a price policy which does not support high cost producers. Government rice policy has to be based on the relationship between the level of rice prices and the income of *full-time* rice growers. In determining the support level the government also has to take into account the difference between domestic and international prices.

c. The use of state-trading should be re-examined. Since state-trading in farm products has not been subjected to serious negotiations in GATT the government is inclined to be mild in asking producers of state-traded commodities to increase productivity. Japanese agricultural policy depends too much on state-trading. While we acknowledge the fact that the Staple Food Control Program established during the war has adjusted to the rapidly changing Japanese food economy since 1955, we believe that further adjustment is needed. For example, barley is not used for direct human consumption in present-day Japan. Only by tradition has barley remained under the Staple Food Control Program until now. Barley could be put under a deficiency payment system. In the same sense trade in dairy products should be re-examined.

B. FAMINE CONDITIONS IN AFRICA AND FOOD AID

In 1985 the attention of the world has been focussed on the terrible famine conditions that exist in and around Ethiopia and, to a lesser degree, in some other areas of Africa. Except for Africa, there has been significant improvement in per capita food availability in the developing world over the past two decades. The progress that has been made in Asia, with its dense and rapidly growing population, supports the view that improvement is possible in the poorest countries. The great reduction in the low income developing countries in infant mortality and the significant increase (16 years) in life expectancy at birth between 1960 and 1982 testifies to the substantial improvement in the food supply, sanitation and other factors affecting the quality of life. Even in Africa infant mortality has been reduced and life expectancy at birth increased by 10 years to 48 years since 1960.

It is important that the current sad situation in parts of Africa be put in proper perspective. It is true that for two or three years the weather has been adverse. But the present shortage of food can hardly be blamed primarily upon adverse weather conditions. In most of sub-Saharan Africa per capita food production has been declining since 1970. During the 1960s, per capita food production was nearly constant, but neglect of agriculture and its exploitation through low prices eventually had adverse effects upon food production.

It is in Ethiopia that the greatest number of unfortunate people have faced famine, and all too many have perished from the combined onslaught of malnutrition and disease. But it must be noted that between 1970 and 1981—before drought hit the region—per capita food production had declined by 15 percent, and that even with normal climatic conditions the food situation had become quite precarious. Had food production in Ethiopia increased at the same rate as in much more densely populated South Asia since 1970, it would have been possible for most people to have withstood the recent drought conditions with a minimum of hardship. But more than a decade of policies inhibiting agricultural production—collectivization, state farms, heavy taxation of export crops, and concentration of investment in urban areas—took their toll. As if these ill-founded policies were not enough, more than a decade of civil war and strife have added immeasurably to the misery of millions.

Massive relief and aid efforts are now underway. Some of the efforts are designed to provide food to prevent further misery and starvation; other efforts are to rebuild and reinvigorate production of food. However, there are two major cautions that must be stated. The first is that the trilateral countries must take extreme care that their deliveries of food do not arrive at a time that farm prices in the affected areas will be adversely affected—particularly at harvest time. Given the delays that now seem to be occurring in the delivery of food aid, there is a real

danger that some of the food aid will worsen the economic circum-
stances of many farm people. It is all too easy to assume that delivering
food to hungry people can only have favorable outcomes but food aid
must be managed with great care if the harm is not to exceed the
benefit. In particular, the trilateral countries must not use the current
food shortages in Africa as an excuse to dispose of unwanted surpluses
of farm products that have been accumulated as a result of their price
support policies.

The second caution is that private and public aid efforts will be for
naught unless the farm and food policies of most African nations are
substantially modified to provide farmers with adequate production
incentives. Production incentives include not only reasonable prices
for what farmers produce but also the availability of farm inputs on
reasonable terms. All too many farm areas in Africa still lack access to
urban markets due to the absence of roads or any other form of low cost
transportation. To some considerable degree, the food shortages in
African countries other than Ethiopia are a consequence of limited
transportation availability.

There is general agreement that Africa has the natural resources for a
substantial and sustained increase in agricultural production, but it
will not be easy to correct past policy errors and rebuild the confidence
of farm people so that they can be in command of their own fate and
become once again productive members of the world economy and no
longer the object of charity. Experience in other areas of the world, in
Asia in particular, indicates that such expectations can be realized.

C. NEW GATT NEGOTIATIONS

We actively support agricultural negotiations in the new GATT Round
now taking shape. At many points throughout this report we have
stressed the importance of the trilateral countries moving together
toward greater market orientation, and the occasion of multilateral
negotiations provides a framework to encourage realization of these
mutual gains.

As this is written, the scope and nature of the negotiation are not
clear. The GATT Committee on Trade in Agriculture (CTA) is to submit
its report in November, and important questions remain unsettled.

The strengthening of GATT rules should be the first order of business. We noted earlier that the GATT article on "General Elimination of
Quantitive Restrictions"—Article XI—has been widely ignored; and
the minimum objective of negotiations on the import barriers side
should be to bring about a higher degree of observance of its provi-

sions, including those with respect to minimum access. The critical first step is for the United States to give up the waiver of Article XI obligations it obtained in 1955 and has maintained ever since. Import quotas have been the method used by the United States to protect some of its price support programs, especially for wheat, dairy products, peanuts, and cotton. The levy approach has been used by the European Community.

This U.S. step would have major symbolic as well as substantive importance, given the historical role of the American waiver in undermining efforts to come to grips with agriculture in the GATT. In practical terms, such a move by the United States has become easier with the application since 1984 of restrictions on the domestic production of dairy products, which could potentially bring this most prominent of U.S. import quotas into compliance with Article XI provisions.

The United States giving up the waiver would obviously mean that the United States would bring U.S. import quotas within the discipline of Article XI. Likewise if the Community would bring the operation of the variable levy within a reasonable interpretation of permitted Article XI exceptions, and if Japan were to make the operation of its state-trading agencies and its quantitative restrictions subject to GATT review, substantial progress could be made. The most relevant Article XI exception is that which permits import restrictions "necessary to the enforcement of governmental measures which operate to restrict the quantities of the like domestic product permitted to be marketed or produced." Article XI goes on to say that import restrictions permitted under this exception

> shall not be such as will reduce the total of imports relative to the total of domestic production, as compared with the proportion which might reasonably be expected to rule between the two in the absence of restrictions. In determining this proportion, the contracting party shall pay due regard to the proportion prevailing during a previous representative period and to any special factors which may have affected or may be affecting the trade in the product concerned.

Strengthened observance of Article XI should include a reasonably common interpretation of what this exception allows. The use of quantitative import restrictions—including variable levies and state-trading measures as well as explicit import quotas—should not be permitted to impede the move to market-oriented policies. Negotiations should consider the level of protection and access that is provided by quantitative import controls as an appropriate topic for discussion. Given the dynamic nature of agricultural markets, the use of a representative period for determining acceptable levels of imports will frustrate efforts to reduce protection of agriculture. At a minimum, when governments use import quotas or similar devices they should be required to substantiate the conformity of their domestic supply program to the provisions of Article XI. Canada is the only trilateral country that—with some exceptions—has taken its obligations under Article XI seriously in the past.

Turning from import restrictions to GATT rules on export subsidies, we noted earlier in our report that subsidies seem not to have been restrained by even the mild exhortations of Article XVI. There have been efforts over time to elaborate the single paragraph that constituted Article XVI in the original General Agreement. Several "Additional Provisions on Export Subsidies" were added in the 1950s, and one of the codes which emerged from the Tokyo Round—the Code on Subsidies and Countervailing Duties—added considerably more detail. (The European Community, Canada, the United States, and Japan have all accepted this Code, though many other contracting parties have not.) Nevertheless an effective regime has not been established—as the running dispute between the Community and the United States indicates. Some panels established under the Code have been unable to agree on what it means in particular cases. The exception to the general prohibition of subsidies on exports is stated in Section B, Paragraph 3 of Article XVI:

> Accordingly, contracting parties should seek to avoid the use of subsidies on the export of primary products. If, however, a contracting party grants directly or indirectly any form of subsidy which operates to increase the export of any primary product from its territory, such subsidy shall not be applied in a manner which results in that contracting party having more than an equitable share of world export trade in that product, account being taken of the shares of the contracting parties in such trade in the product during a previous representative period, and any special factors which may have affected or may be affecting such trade in the product.

The GATT Committee has been addressing the subsidy and export credit issues. We support an active effort to extend and tighten GATT rules against subsidies. United States willingness to bring export credits and other forms of assistance which operate like export subsidies under the framework of improved GATT rules on export subsidies and all other forms of export assistance should encourage other trilateral countries to be more forthcoming as well. Strengthened rules against subsidies would recognize that a time of adjustment is required. Some exceptions would be necessary, perhaps along the lines of and in symmetry with the exceptions granted in Article XI for quantitative restrictions, strictly interpreted.

The present situation of agriculture in GATT has developed largely as a result of there being no effective limits on the effects of domestic support policies on trade. Contracting parties are unwilling to accept that domestic policies as such could be negotiated directly with other countries. The international handle on these policies is their impact on trading partners, and thus the aim of negotiations is to constrain and reduce the trade effects of national farm programs that distort agricultural production and trade. The task is to devise a set of commitments, rules and arrangements which will require countries to modify their national farm policies in ways that contribute to the overall objectives of the agricultural negotiations, but without requiring them to make explicitly negotiated and legally-binding changes in the fundamental objectives of their policies, the instruments which are used, or the character and coverage of national programs, regulations and institutional arrangements. To be sure there will be some specific and legally binding commitments that will necessarily translate into changes in the parameters of national farm programs, but the manner in which national farm programs are adapted to incorporate such obligations has not yet been fully considered in GATT negotiations. The aim is to channel national farm policies into more internationally constructive directions rather than to negotiate the content of such policies directly.

Whereas traditional trade negotiations have been concerned to reach a balanced set of *reciprocal concessions* on access to import markets, the new negotiations will need to combine this with *mutual limitations* on the use of import restrictions and export subsidies, export credits, and other forms of export assistance under strengthened GATT rules, and *contributions* to international market stability. The acceptance of multilateral constraints and obligations on the conduct of national farm policies and associated agricultural trade regimes will permit national authorities to effect a "disarmament of protection"—a mutual de-escalation in their contending and defensive farm programs and agricultural trade practices, and provide welcome opportunities to curb expenditures on them. Because of the tension between some trilateral countries, it would be more useful to separate the strengthening and improvement of GATT rules and the negotiations on further liberalization of agricultural trade.

It is important that agricultural negotiations take place in the framework of a larger trade negotiation effort. One often overlooked reason for this is that, if agricultural policy regimes are to be adjusted to a more market-oriented basis, the negotiations must reverse the recent trends toward increased protection of manufactured products. In particular, the adjustments required of agriculture will be reduced if the developing countries, especially the rapidly growing ones, are given reasonable access in the markets of the industrial countries for their manufactured products. The most significant potential for expansion of markets for farm products is in such rapidly growing countries. The growth of that market depends importantly upon their ability to pay. We cannot emphasize too strongly that protection of manufactured products, especially in steel, automobiles and textiles and other labor-intensive manufactured products has imposed significant economic burdens upon agriculture through increasing costs and limiting export markets.

Of course, for those developing countries which cannot export the above-mentioned manufactured products, access to our markets for such products as sugar or foods on which they have a comparative advantage is a key to their sound economic development. This is an area where the trilateral countries can contribute to the solution of one of the most important world issues in recent years. Moreover, these developing countries can be a promising future market for our farm products.

Finally, what has always been lacking in past GATT rounds is the political will to come to grips with the distortions that permeate agricultural production and trade, to qualify freedom of national farm policies, and to accept legally binding multilateral constraints on the trade effects of these policies. That political will may still be missing today, but the chances of progress seem better than ever before. The United States is more aware of the costs of its policies and more willing to acknowledge its own faults. The European Community is also more aware of the costs of its policies, and its perspective is changing as its historical situation shifts from that of an importer seeking to expand domestic production to that of a major exporter of temperate agricultural products. Japan is greatly concerned with the health of the overall international trading system and more aware of its own leadership role. Canada, which is deeply dependent on a well-functioning world food market, is well aware of the need to make adjustments to its own agricultural programs that subsidize high cost national production and contribute to the distortions in the food production and trading system. The new GATT Round provides an opportunity which should not be lost.

Appendix

Appendix

This appendix is divided into six parts. Essays on agricultural policies in the United States, Canada, the European Community and Japan constitute Sections A-D—essays from which much of Chapter I of the foregoing report was drawn. These four essays were individually authored. The essay on Canada was taken from longer paper prepared for the project by T. K. Warley. The Japan essay was prepared by Kenzo Hemmi, the U.S. essay by D. Gale Johnson, and the essay on the Common Agricultural Policy by Pierre Lardinois along with P. A. J. Wijnmaalen and Bram Kruimel. We have not tried to standardize these four essays, each written in its own way; but they do have some common elements. A table presenting the evolution of some key indicators over the past two decades is presented in each—Tables US-6, CN-2, EC-1 and JN-1. The U.S. and Japanese essays include similar original tables (Tables US-9 and JN-3) which attempt to estimate consumer as well as taxpayer costs of policies in these two countries.

Appendix Sections E and F provide background for two other parts of the foregoing report. The results of efforts to estimate the effects of domestic protection on international prices are presented in Section E. Data on relative prices received by farmers and rates of decline in farm employment are presented in Section F.

A. UNITED STATES AGRICULTURE AND POLICY

The agricultural policy of the United States has many facets. At the very general level, its objective is to provide farm people with the same opportunities to share in the growth of income of the economy as the rest of the nation's people. For a very long time, policymakers have maintained their confidence in the role that research and education could play in improving the economic lot of the farmer. Other broad policies have included such measures as the development of a rural road system, a rural electrification network to serve all farm families, the creation of a credit system to serve the particular needs of farmers, and a rural postal service and telephones that provide farm people ready access to the knowledge, goods and services available to urban people.

But these broad policies, which have their counterparts in all industrial market economies, are not the ones that directly influence current production, prices and consumption and the flow of international trade in farm products. Measures of income support are the principal policies that actually or potentially affect consumer and producer prices, the level of production, and the necessity to intervene in the flow of farm products across national boundaries. Income support can take many forms—price supports, intervention prices, target prices and deficiency payments, two-price systems, and input subsidies are the most important ones.

Farm Programs in the 1980s
As this text is completed in August 1985, the Food and Agricultural Act of 1981 is the authority for most interventions designed to influence prices, production and incomes. The legislation established minimum price support levels for 1982 through 1985 for wheat, feed grains, dairy products, cotton, rice, soybeans, peanuts, and sugar. The soybean price support was set at a level expected to be well below actual market prices,

and this has proved to be the case. The same cannot be said about the other price supports, however. Each one has resulted in farmers obtaining nonrecourse loans on significant amounts of products and in the government (through the Commodity Credit Corporation) acquiring substantial quantities of wheat, feed grains, dairy products, cotton and rice.

In addition to the price supports, target prices were provided in the 1981 legislation for wheat, feed grains, cotton and rice (see Table US-1). The target prices do not directly affect market prices—if market prices are below the target prices the difference is paid to the producer by the government in the form of a deficiency payment. However, the levels of the target prices can and do influence farmers' production decisions. If the target prices are set significantly above what the market prices would be in the absence of governmental intervention, then incentives are created for increasing output.

Farmers have been required to participate in supply management programs to obtain the deficiency payments associated with the target prices and to have access to farm price support loans. However, in some years the acreage limitations were modest and had limited effect upon output. In the 1980s only the massive Payment-in-Kind (PIK) program—under which, in return for reducing acreage, farmers were paid in kind a high percentage of their normal yields—in 1983 had a measurable impact upon agricultural output. The PIK program, which idled about a quarter of all cropland, was instituted to reduce the available stocks of grain and cotton, to strengthen market prices, and to lower governmental costs for storage and deficiency payments. To some degree, supply management efforts are required to offset the output effects of target prices and price supports.

The Agricultural Act of 1981 and the previous legislation have not been successful in meeting the changing conditions facing U.S. agriculture. Net farm operator income in 1983 was more than a quarter lower than in the previous year and barely more than half the 1981 level. Crop output was at high levels in 1981 and 1982, resulting in substantial increases of U.S. stocks of feed grains and wheat. In particular, recent legislation has failed to a considerable degree to move U.S. agriculture toward greater market orientation. From the late 1950s through the 1970s the general trend of farm policy was to move away from substantial governmental involvement in the markets for farm products and to give a greater role to the markets to determine what was produced, how the available output was allocated between current utilization and stocks, and how the current use was distributed between domestic and export sales. Export subsidies, which had been used to a considerable degree in the disposal of wheat and cotton during the 1950s and 1960s, were discontinued in the early 1970s. Limited use of direct export subsidies re-emerged in 1983. In recent years, subsidized credit to finance exports has been a limited form of export subsidization; the amount of the subsidy on commercial sales is limited by the smallness of the interest rate differential.

The Evolution of Farm Programs
At the end of World War II there was a major debate in the United States concerning farm policy. One important group wanted to largely eliminate the government as a major factor in agricultural production and marketing, and argued that price supports should be set at "stop loss" levels. In other words, the government was to step in only when there was a temporary downswing in farm prices with the expectation that within a relatively short period of time prices would recover to more satisfactory levels. The second group argued, apparently in part on the assumption that there would be a major depression in agriculture after World War II just as there was after World War I, that farmers could not rely upon the market to absorb the output they could produce at acceptable prices.

TABLE US-1

Target Prices, Loan Rates and Prices Received by Farmers in the United States, 1974-85

| Year | WHEAT | | | CORN | | | RICE | | | COTTON | | | MILK[a] | |
| | Target Price | Loan Rate | Price Received | Target Price | Loan Rate | Price Received | Target Price | Loan Rate | Price Received | Target Price | Loan Rate | Price Received | Price Support | Price Received |
	($ per metric ton)			($ per metric ton)			($ per metric ton)			(cents per lb.)			($ per metric ton)	
1974/75	75.23	50.28	150.10	54.30	43.28	118.84	—	166.18	251.26	38.0	27.1	42.7	145	157
1975/76	75.23	50.28	130.65	54.30	43.28	99.95	—	187.78	184.03	38.0	36.1	51.1	160	168
1976/77	84.04	85.58	100.19	61.78	59.02	84.60	181.83	136.43	154.73	43.2	38.9	63.8	179	189
1977/78	106.43	85.58	85.51	78.70	78.70	79.49	181.83	136.43	209.16	47.8	44.6	52.1	198	192
1978/79	124.78	86.24	109.00	82.64	78.70	88.54	188.00	141.06	179.84	52.0	48.0	58.1	218	214
1979/80	124.78	91.75	138.73	86.57	82.64	99.16	199.46	149.65	231.42	57.7	50.2	62.3	253	245
1980/81	133.22	110.1	143.50	92.47	88.54	122.38	209.16	156.92	282.11	58.4	48.0	74.4	288	264
1981/82	139.82	117.44	133.96	94.44	94.44	98.38	235.39	176.54	199.46	70.9	52.5	54.0	291	280
1982/83	148.63	130.29	130.28	106.24	100.34	105.46	239.13	179.41	178.74	71.0	57.1	59.1	289	280
1983/84	157.81	133.96	129.92	112.54	104.28	127.89	251.26	179.41	187.34	76.0	55.0	66.1	286	278
1984/85	160.75	121.1	—	119.23	100.34	—	262.28	176.32	—	81.0	55.0	—		
1985/86	160.75	121.1	—	119.23	100.34	—	262.28	176.32	—			—		

[a]Data are for calendar years; first year in table is 1974. The price supports are approximate averages for a year.

Consequently the policies adopted during World War II of using relatively high price supports to encourage farmers to expand production should be continued to protect farmers from the adverse economic conditions that it was assumed would prevail.

For a time it appeared that the first group had won. The Agricultural Act of 1948 provided for price supports that were relatively low and flexible downward as well as upward. However, the presidential election of 1948 intervened and new farm legislation—the Agricultural Act of 1949—represented a sharp turn toward the retention of relatively high price supports. It was the Act of 1949 that guided farm policy during the early 1950s and resulted in very large stocks of farm products accumulated as a result of price support operations. The domestic prices were too high to permit sufficient exports without export subsidies. One tentative answer to the excess productive capacity of U.S. agriculture was food aid, which was made available in large amounts throughout most of the 1950s and early 1960s following the legislation (PL 480) passed in 1954. But even large scale food aid shipments and efforts at supply management were inadequate to dispose of the available output at prices that would provide reasonable incomes for farm people.

It became apparent that U.S. agriculture had excess resources—there were more resources (labor, land and capital) engaged in farming than could earn acceptable incomes or returns. It was then that the decision was made to move toward greater market orientation through significant reductions in price supports. By the mid-1960s the price supports for wheat and corn, after adjustment for inflation, were about half of what they were in 1950-54 (Table US-2). The responses to the lower price supports were a significant growth in exports and a gradual adjustment in resources in agriculture, especially labor through transfer to non-farm jobs. Production costs declined as a result of steady growth in productivity and the returns to farm labor increased in spite of the significant decline in output prices in real terms.

By the early 1970s almost all of the excess resources had been removed from U.S. agriculture. While the governmental expenditures on farm price support and income stabilization programs in real terms remained at high levels until 1974, these expenditures were not a good indication of how far the adjustment had gone (Table US-3). By the early 1970s, the acreage limitation programs—still an important part of expenditures— had little effect upon total farm production, resulting in a reduction of no more than 2 percent. Another factor causing large governmental payments during the early 1970s was the need to reduce inventories of farm products accumulated by the Commodity Credit Corporation during the late 1960s. But the most important factor was the overvaluation of the dollar which depressed U.S. farm prices, then as now. The prices of major export crops were depressed by about 10 percent by the overvaluation of the dollar and the resulting reduction in farm income was approximately equal to the net income from the governmental payments. The governmental payments that were retained as net income by farmers were no more than half of the amount actually received.[1]

With the sharp increase in farm prices in late 1972 and 1973 the withdrawal of resources from agriculture was halted and there was a substantial increase in capital invested in agriculture, fostered in part by favorable tax treatment as well as by the very high incomes of the larger commercial farmers in 1973 and 1974 and lower but still high incomes from 1975 through 1979 (except for 1977).

---

[1]For a more complete exposition of these points, see D. Gale Johnson, "Resource Adjustments in American Agriculture and Agricultural Policy," in William Fellner, editor, *Contemporary Economic Problems 1977* (Washington, D.C.: American Enterprise Institute, 1977), pp. 216-19. It was also emphasized in this article that a large fraction of the payments resulting in an increase in net farm income went to increasing land values, while the income going to capital and labor was affected rather little.

TABLE US-2

U.S. Price Support or Loan Rates, 1950-84
(in 1982 dollars)

YEAR	WHEAT ($/MT)	CORN ($/MT)	SOYBEANS ($/MT)	MANUFACTURED MILK ($/MT)	COTTON (cents/kg)
1950	282.68	224.57	291.32	261.33	257.22
51	290.38	223.54	325.94	287.86	258.53
52	289.41	224.57	336.51	303.43	255.65
53	285.56	221.48	330.75	290.17	259.58
54	285.56	221.48	282.68	241.13	260.10
1955	259.60	211.17	254.79	236.52	259.05
56	242.28	194.71	260.57	233.07	237.60
57	233.65	176.16	244.22	228.44	227.39
58	209.60	167.91	241.34	211.72	242.83
59	203.84	134.94	207.69	206.54	230.27
1960	197.09	125.68	204.78	205.96	215.09
61	196.15	141.12	251.91	223.83	217.45
62	215.38	138.03	242.28	200.75	209.86
63	193.24	121.55	238.43	199.60	206.46
64	135.57	122.59	234.59	197.30	188.14
1965	127.88	115.37	229.80	198.45	177.67
66	124.03	106.11	247.09	222.68	124.55
67	120.19	108.17	240.37	230.74	116.44
68	115.37	104.04	229.80	236.52	111.99
69	109.61	98.89	197.09	224.98	106.24
1970	103.83	93.76	187.49	232.49	101.00
71	99.04	88.60	177.88	234.22	92.89
72	95.20	85.51	171.13	224.98	88.97
73	89.41	80.36	161.53	236.52	84.26
74	90.38	78.29	148.08	260.18	99.70
1975	82.69	71.07	—	262.48	124.03
76	128.85	92.71	143.26	280.96	127.96
77	122.10	116.42	190.36	293.04	138.42
78	119.22	108.17	227.86	299.40	145.49
79	116.34	105.09	209.60	320.76	140.26
1980	127.88	103.02	213.44	327.09	122.98
81	125.00	94.78	195.18	305.74	122.98
82	130.76	99.93	184.61	288.44	125.86
83	128.85	99.93	176.92	276.90	116.44
84	112.49	92.91	170.90	—	112.50

MT = metric ton

Source: United States Department of Agriculture, *Agricultural Statistics*, annual issues. Deflated by U.S. Wholesale Price Index.

Price supports were increased substantially in 1976 and 1978 (see Table US-2 above). Stocks of farm commodities reached burdensome levels by the end of 1979 in spite of modest efforts at supply management in 1978 and 1979. In fact, U.S. stocks of feed grains in 1979/80 exceeded the high levels of the late 1960s and wheat stocks reached the levels of a decade earlier as well.

The Agricultural Act of 1981 set target prices and price supports that at the time were believed to be at reasonable levels. In part this view of the prices in the 1981 Act (which instead resulted in record levels of grain stocks within two years) was based on the mistaken view that world demand for farm products would grow at a more rapid rate than supply. Instead the contrary occurred. Demand grew more slowly than supply. The 1981 Act included no provision for downward adjustment of price support levels for the grains. The administration did not help matters by establishing the reserve loan levels for wheat and corn in 1981 and 1982 at levels higher than required by the legislation.

It was clearly an error not to provide for downward adjustment of price support and target price levels in the 1981 legislation. Congress was unwilling until 1984 to modify the minimum price supports, set in advance for four years, or the target prices which had been set for the same time period. The 1984 target price for wheat was reduced by less than 2 percent; the 1985 target price was reduced by 6 percent. The 1985 corn target price was reduced by about 5 percent. However, these adjustments seem too modest to have any significant effect in reducing excess supplies.

United States agriculture has been affected to a very important degree, as was noted above, by variations in the foreign exchange value of the dollar. The rapid growth of agricultural exports after 1972 was due in considerable part to the fall in the value of the dollar by about a fourth between 1971 and 1980. Similarly, the slowdown in export growth and the actual decline that occurred in 1981 and 1982 was due at least in part to the rise in the value of the dollar, which by 1983 had recovered to the same level as 1971. The recession that affected most industrial economies and the debt problems of many developing countries also contributed to the slow growth and decline of U.S. agricultural exports after 1980. But these external factors would have had significantly smaller effects upon the volume of U.S. agricultural exports had price supports been at lower levels and if the efforts at output reduction in the United States had not been anticipated by other countries that expanded their production levels to take advantage of the expected higher price.

The decline in exports associated with high price supports (so high as to make the United States a residual supplier) can have long run as well as short run effects. This is clearly illustrated by the U.S. tobacco program. The tobacco program has been successful in increasing both domestic and world market prices of tobacco through effective control of U.S. output over the past four decades. In recent years, in contrast to almost all other crops, output levels have been no more than two decades ago and in some years significantly smaller. While the U.S. held up world prices, its share of world production of flue-cured tobacco (the principal type of export tobacco) fell from 64 percent in 1935-39 to 18 percent in 1980-82; the U.S. share of world exports declined from 83 percent to 21 percent over the same period.[2]

One may doubt that anyone anticipated that one consequence of the tobacco program would be that the United States would become the world's largest importer of tobacco.

[2]James A. Seagraves, "The Life-cycle of the Flue-cured Tobacco Program," Working Paper No. 34, Department of Economics and Business, North Carolina State University, March 1983, p. 28. See also, Daniel A. Sumner and Julian M. Alston, "Consequences of Elimination of the Tobacco Program," North Carolina Agricultural Research Service, North Carolina State University, Bul. 469, March 1984.

TABLE US-3

**U.S. Federal Governmental Expenditures upon Farm Price Supports and
Income Stabilization, 1950-83**

Fiscal Year	Current Dollars	1982 Dollars
1950	1,845	7,126
51	−461	−1,670
52	45	161
53	2,125	7,474
54	1,688	5,865
55	3,378	11,486
1956	3,330	10,972
57	2,174	6,926
58	2,078	6,510
59	4,104	12,558
60	2,046	6,161
1961	2,346	7,001
62	3,093	9,062
63	3,693	10,661
64	4,144	11,783
65	3,438	9,566
1966	1,925	5,189
67	2,529	6,617
68	3,934	9,860
69	5,047	12,031
70	4,676	10,579
1971	3,633	7,828
72	5,015	10,374
73	4,678	9,151
74	1,364	2,452
75	918	1,510
1976	1,278	1,998
77	4,092	6,044
78	5,935	8,163
79	3,833	4,853
80	2,981	3,457
1981	4,221	4,475
82	11,919	11,919
83	19,220	18,440[a]

[a]Preliminary GNP deflator for 1983.

Source: Willard W. Cochrane and Mary E. Ryan, *American Farm Policy* (Minneapolis: University of Minnesota Press, 1976), and The Budget of the United States. The deflator is from *The Economic Report of the President*, 1984.

The high U.S. prices of tobacco combined with poundage output allotments to U.S. producers has meant that farmers have emphasized high quality tobacco and have foregone the production of low quality tobacco. Net tobacco exports have declined by half since the early 1960s.

In the case of tobacco the United States has not limited imports by quantitative restrictions nor have export subsidies been used during the past decade (and before that only quite briefly and at moderate levels). The tobacco program has continued to receive support from farmers because the quotas that one must have to produce tobacco have substantial value and abolishing the tobacco program would result in substantial losses to the current owners of the quotas. The value of tobacco quotas for the production of a hectare of tobacco land is approximately $2,200 per year; this is not the capital value but the value of one year's use or rental of the quota. For countries considering the adoption of output quotas as a means of reducing governmental costs of farm price supports, it is relevant to note that less than a third of the tobacco quotas are owned by farmers now growing tobacco. If quotas are transferable, either directly or with the sale or rental of land or animals, it will not be many years before most of the benefits from quota schemes go to quota owners who are landlords or others who are not engaged in actual farm operations.

One facet of U.S. crop programs has only been noted, namely the removal of cropland from cultivation. Table US-4 indicates the acres of cropland that have been idled since the mid-1950s. The total amount of cropland harvested in 1980 and 1981, when there were no programs to idle farm land, was approximately 350 million acres (142 million hectares). It is clear that in some years a substantial percentage of cropland was idled under the farm programs. The first column shows the value in 1983 dollars of crop inventories and loans held by the Commodity Credit Corporation. In the 1950s and 1960s these were very large and became so again in 1983.

Effects of U.S. Farm Programs on Foreign Trade

The exceptions written into the GATT that permit the use of quantitative restrictions on imports of agricultural products were devised by the United States to obtain acceptance of the GATT by Congress. But these exceptions were not sufficient to permit the United States to carry out some of its farm programs. In particular, the United States has long had a dairy price support program, with domestic prices at levels in excess of international prices. Import quotas were imposed even though the conditions required by Article XI of the GATT were not met. (No effort was made to restrict dairy production—a key condition—until 1984.) In 1951 the United States was found to be guilty of an "infringement" of Article XI. Later the basic U.S. Agricultural Adjustment Act of 1933 was amended by Section 22, legislation that required the administration to impose quantitative restrictions or special fees (above and beyond customs duties) whenever "any article or articles are being or are practically certain to be imported into the United States under such conditions and in such quantities as to render or tend to render ineffective or materially interfere with" any U.S. farm program. Interference was interpreted broadly to include significantly increasing the cost of the program to the Treasury.

The existence of Section 22 made it necessary for the United States in 1955 to request a waiver from GATT from the provisions of Article XI. It obtained a waiver which had no time limit and did not include any commitment from the United States to modify its legislation and farm programs so that it could live within the exceptions provided in Article XI. The United States has done little or nothing to modify its domestic programs so that it could release the waiver and live within the exceptions. In fact, in 1964 legislation was passed permitting the imposition of import quotas on beef, veal and lamb when imports exceeded a specified level. This legislation made no pretense of abiding by the GATT rules. There was not then and there is not now any domestic program limiting the production of meat in the United States. It is true that the legislation provided for importers to share in the growth of the U.S. market, but otherwise there was not the slightest nod to the GATT principles.

For nearly four decades, ending in 1974, the United States sugar program provided for limiting domestic production of sugar. For the next four years the U.S. had no import quotas on sugar, but various measures to limit imports, including import quotas, were reimposed in 1979. The current sugar program has no provision for limiting domestic production of sugar and thus maintaining a given share of total consumption for imports.

Even before 1974 when the United States had a program that purportedly restricted domestic output of sugar it did not abide by the GATT guideline for the use of import quotas. This guideline states that when quantitative restrictions are used in conjunction with a domestic output limitation program, the quota " ...shall not be such as will reduce the total of imports relative to the total domestic production as compared with the proportion which might reasonably be expected to rule between the two in the absence of

TABLE US-4

Indicators of U.S. Government Intervention in Agriculture, Fiscal Years 1956-83

Year	Commodity Loans and Inventory (in billions of 1983 dollars)[a]	Acreage Idled Under Government Programs (in millions)[b]
1956-60 average	24.7	24
1961-65 average	22.4	52
1966-70 average	11.9	54
1971	11.3	38
1972	7.4	62
1973	7.6	20
1974	3.2	3
1975	1.1	2
1976	1.2	2
1977	1.8	1
1978	6.1	18
1979	7.3	13
1980	6.1	—
1981	8.7	—
1982	9.2	11.1
1983	16.9	77

[a]Total value of outstanding commodity price support loans and government-owned inventories at start of the fiscal year.

[b]Acreage idled in calendar year in which fiscal year ends.

Source: U.S. Department of Agriculture and the Congressional Budget Office.

restrictions." It is suggested that the proportion between imports and domestic production that prevailed "during a previous representative period" should apply unless there are special factors that make that period unrepresentative.

If 1925-29 were considered to be the representative period prior to the enactment of sugar legislation in 1934, the sugar programs failed to meet the guideline. In 1925-29 sugar imports were 1.7 times as large as domestic production; by 1970 sugar imports were only 0.81 times as large as domestic production. Under the present sugar program, sugar imports are about 0.5 times domestic production. However, this comparison is unduly favorable to the current sugar program. Because of the high domestic price of sugar, other caloric sweeteners have captured a substantial share of the sweetener market. Sweeteners made primarily from corn now account for more than a third of all caloric sweeteners used in the United States and in 1983 and 1984 exceeded the quantity of U.S. sugar imports. The production of caloric sweeteners from grain has been encouraged by the high domestic price for sugar, which as of early 1985 was about five times the world market price.

A modest production diversion or reduction program for milk was instituted in 1984, as noted above. This was the first time in almost 50 years that dairy import quotas have been imposed that the United States has met even one of the exceptions of Article XI, namely that domestic output be reduced to maintain imports' share of the market. Due to the heavy costs of dairy price supports in recent years, a serious effort is being made to reduce dairy production to the level of domestic use. However, there is no indication that the intention is to determine if the U.S. producers could compete in international markets.

It is probable that if the United States eliminated its price supports for dairy products and permitted imports with nominal import duties, there would be significant imports of dairy products. However, dairy production is so seriously distorted by the policies of the United States, the European Community, Japan, and Canada that it is not possible without a great deal of analysis to determine what would happen to world trade in dairy products if there were general liberalization of trade by OECD countries.

The United States now has a two price system for peanuts, made possible by a very restrictive import quota. Peanuts consumed as peanuts or peanut butter have a price support that is above the international market price. These peanuts are limited by a production quota; other peanuts can be produced freely but at a price approximately equal to the world market price. Such peanuts are either exported or crushed for oil and meal.

The 1964 law that permits import quotas on beef has never been directly implemented; instead the United States has used the law to induce the major exporters to accept voluntary restraints upon their beef and veal exports to the U.S. The degree of restraint has been quite modest and in approximately half of the years since 1970 the anticipated level of beef and veal imports was less than what was permitted under the law and the voluntary quotas were not negotiated. Even when the restraints are in effect, the impact upon either imports or the level of U.S. beef prices has been quite modest. The continued existence of the quota law is hard to justify given its limited effect upon beef prices and the barrier that it presents in negotiating reductions in protection for farm products.

While the United States objects to the payment of export subsidies by others, the deficiency payments associated with the target prices have some of the same effects as export subsidies. As a part of supply management programs various other payments are also made. Table US-5 shows the importance of such payments, including deficiency payments, for the period from 1968/69 to date. For the feed grains the payments were quite modest from 1974/75 to 1982/83; in only one of these years did the payments amount to as much as 5 percent of the price received by farmers. However, a combination of drastically reduced areas devoted to feed grains in 1983 and a severe drought caused the payments for 1983/84 to equal nearly 45 percent of the farm price.

Payments to wheat producers were a relatively small percentage of the farm price for all years from 1974/75 through 1982/83 except for 1977/78 and 1978/79 when the payments averaged 21 and 15 percent of the price respectively. In 1983/84 the wheat payments were very large compared to the farm price.

As noted the target price has some of the same effects as export subsidies. One important difference is that the domestic price remains at the same level as the export or world price; consequently, domestic consumption is not reduced by the target price as it is when domestic market prices are increased by interventions. But both target prices and export subsidies induce increased production (when the target price exceeds the market

TABLE US-5

**U.S. Market Prices, Supplementary Payments and Export Subsidies
for Wheat and Feed Grains, 1968/69-1983/84**
($ per metric ton)

	WHEAT			FEED GRAINS		
YEAR	PRICES RECEIVED BY FARMERS	AVERAGE PAYMENT ON ALL WHEAT	EXPORT SUBSIDY	PRICES RECEIVED BY FARMERS FOR CORN	AVERAGE PAYMENT ON ALL FEED GRAINS	EXPORT SUBSIDY
1968/69	45.56	17.68	—	39.68	8.84	—
1969/70	45.56	21.88	5.51	45.67	10.22	0.12
1970/71	48.86	23.65	8.45	52.36	10.39	0.61
1971/72	49.23	20.11	5.14	42.52	5.62	0.50
1972/73	64.66	21.04	9.38	61.81	10.27	—
1973/74	145.12	10.21	1.41[a]	100.39	6.28	—
1974/75	150.27	2.10	—	119.29	2.18	—
1975/76	130.79	0.88	—	100.00	0.62	—
1976/77	100.30	2.49	—	84.60	1.16	—
1977/78	104.40	22.32	—	79.50	2.81	—
1978/79	120.50	16.77	—	88.54	4.62	—
1979/80	138.72	2.32	—	99.16	1.04	—
1980/81	146.80	5.28	—	122.38	2.08	—
1981/82	133.96	8.18	—	98.38	1.70	—
1982/83	129.55	8.52	—	105.46	1.65	—
1983/84	129.92	49.39[b]	—	127.72	56.24[b]	—

[a]The wheat export subsidy program was suspended in August 1972 and no new wheat export subsidy commitments were made, but actual subsidy payments were made when wheat on which there was a subsidy commitment was actually shipped.

[b]The payment rate includes the payment-in-kind (PIK) that farmers received for reducing their production. If only cash payments were included, the payment for wheat was $19.95 per ton and for feed grains was $11.21 per ton.

Sources: *Wheat Situation*, various issues; *Feed Situation*, various issues; *Agricultural Statistics*, 1973, 1977, and 1983.

price or the export subsidy is positive). At least part of the extra production induced by the target price finds its way into export markets and thus has the effect of depressing international market prices. This is the same effect that U.S. government officials object to when export subsidies are used by others.

As Table US-1 above showed, target prices have not provided much incentive for increased corn production since the target price has seldom been above the price farmers receive. Since the target prices were instituted, deficiency payments have been made on just two corn crops—about 1 cent per bushel ($0.40 per ton) in 1978 and a little more than 3 cents per bushel ($1.40 per ton) in 1982. The deficiency payment is determined by the difference between the target price and the average farm price for the first five months of the marketing year or the loan rate, whichever is higher. Thus the amount of the deficiency payment cannot be determined by comparing the average price received for the crop year with the target price.

The deficiency payments have been much more important for wheat than for corn. The reason is that the target price for wheat has been set much higher relative to the loan rate or price support level than was true for corn. In some years the target price and loan rates for corn were the same, such as in 1977 and 1981, and in other years differed by 5 percent or less. However, largely for political reasons, the target price for wheat has exceeded the loan rate for wheat by 20 percent or more in most years. While the loan rate for wheat was reduced in 1984, the target price was increased so that the target price exceeded the loan rate by almost a third; the same relationship prevails in 1985. As noted above, modest downward revisions from the levels set in the Agricultural Act of 1981 were made in the target prices for wheat and corn for 1984 and 1985. The target price for cotton was also reduced slightly from the levels set in the 1981 Act. But many would argue that Congress waited much too long to act and that the downward adjustments were too small—a case of too little too late.

For the grains and cotton the net effect of U.S. farm programs during the 1980s has been to reduce exports. Total grain exports declined from 107 million tons in 1981 to 93 million tons in 1983. This is largely the unintended result of the inflexible price supports and the substantial reduction in farm production achieved by the 1983 PIK program. The U.S. increased its stocks of these commodities rather than exporting them.

Changes in U.S. Agriculture

Before discussing the effects of U.S. farm programs upon the incomes of farm people, it may help to put that discussion in focus with a brief description of changes in U.S. agriculture over the past two decades. As Table US-6 indicates, there were larger changes in agriculture in the 1962-73 period than in the next decade. Employment in agriculture declined by 30 percent from 1962 to 1973 while there was hardly any change during the next decade. The number of farms declined by 23 percent in the first period and by about 15 percent in the second period.

An indication of the increases in productivity is given by the data on production of milk per cow and yields of grain per hectare. In the period of two decades milk output per cow increased by two thirds, the yield of wheat by 41 percent and all grain by 64 percent.

Compared to the European Community and Japan the level of grain yields in the United States is relatively low. As the data on agricultural area and employment in agriculture indicate, in the United States the amount of land per worker is much greater than in Europe or Japan. This is also indicated by the average size of farms since the number of workers per farm is very similar, falling in the range of 1.4 to 1.5 for both the United States and the European Community and about 1.2 for Japan (with farms of much smaller size than the United States or European Community).

The growth of U.S. agricultural trade was large during the period, even recognizing that the data in the table are in current dollars. Agricultural exports increased more rapidly than did agricultural imports. However, the United States—the world's largest exporter of agricultural products—remains one of the world's largest importers of such products as well.

Effects of U.S. Farm Programs upon Farm Income
An important assumption underlying U.S. farm policies has been that supply management—the limitation of production of major farm crops—could increase farm prices and incomes. This assumption is now subject to considerable dispute. The farm legislation proposed by the Reagan administration in early 1985 looks to the elimination of supply management as a policy tool. The reasons for questioning the effectiveness of supply management in increasing either farm prices or incomes merit serious consideration. Perhaps the most important is that in the absence of use of export subsidies to separate domestic and international prices, the output reductions achieved in the U.S. can increase domestic prices only by increasing international market prices.

Wheat may be used as an example. The United States produces about 15 percent of the world's output. If the U.S. reduces its wheat output by 20 percent, world production would be reduced by just 3 percent—and that would be true only if producers in the rest of the world did not increase their production in the expectation of higher prices. A reduction in world output of 3 percent is not likely to have much effect on international market prices. On the basis of rather extreme assumptions about the responsiveness of international market prices to a change in world production, a reduction of U.S. wheat output by 20 percent would increase international prices by no more than 7.5 percent. The reduction in wheat acreage by the PIK program in 1983 was offset by increases in the

TABLE US-6

Selected Data for U.S. Agriculture, 1962, 1973 and 1983

	1962	1973	1983
Agriculture's share in GDP (%)[b]	3.6	3.8	1.9
Agricultural area (million ha.)[c]	469	441	420
Persons employed (x 1000)[b]	4,944	3,470	3,383
Number of farms (x 1000)[c]	3,692	2,844	2,370
Average hectares per farm[c]	127	155	177
Average production per milk cow (kg/head)[c]	3,353	4,590	5,045
Average production of wheat (100 kg/ha.)[c,d]	16.9	21.2	23.9
Average production of all grain (100 kg/ha.)[a,c]	26.8	37.4	44.1
External trade: exports ($ U.S. billion)[b]	5.0	17.7	36.1
External trade: imports ($ U.S. billion)[b]	3.9	8.4	16.6

[a]Data are for 1982 due to effects of drought and farm programs on yields in 1983.
[b]Taken from *Economic Report of the President*, February 1985.
[c]Taken from U.S. Department of Agriculture, *Agricultural Statistics*, 1983.
[d]Yield per harvested hectare.

TABLE US-7

Per Capita Personal and Disposable Personal Income of U.S. Farm and Nonfarm Populations, 1934-83

YEAR	PER CAPITA PERSONAL INCOME OF FARM POPULATION			PER CAPITA DISPOSABLE PERSONAL INCOME			FARM AS PERCENTAGE OF NONFARM PER CAPITA DISPOSABLE INCOME, ALL SOURCES
	FROM FARM SOURCES[a]	FROM NONFARM SOURCES[b]	FROM ALL SOURCES	OF FARM POPULATION FROM ALL SOURCES	OF NONFARM POPULATION FROM ALL SOURCES	OF TOTAL POPULATION FROM ALL SOURCES	
	(U.S. dollars)						(percent)
1934	99	66	167	163	498	413	32.7
1935	169	72	241	237	534	459	44.4
1936	145	83	228	224	614	517	36.5
1937	199	88	287	283	636	550	44.5
1938	152	80	232	227	588	502	38.6
1939	154	85	239	235	627	534	37.5
1940	159	90	249	240	669	570	35.9
1941	227	108	335	323	798	691	40.5
1942	351	136	487	464	974	865	47.6
1943	463	166	629	555	1,072	973	51.8
1944	491	179	670	593	1,152	1,052	51.5
1945	525	180	705	619	1,160	1,066	53.4
1946	609	179	788	706	1,216	1,124	58.1
1947	613	205	818	726	1,268	1,170	57.3
1948	737	239	976	877	1,363	1,282	64.3
1949	549	256	805	733	1,361	1,259	53.9
1950	611	272	883	802	1,462	1,362	54.9
1951	738	297	1,035	917	1,556	1,465	58.9
1952	703	309	1,012	884	1,616	1,515	54.7
1953	667	324	991	868	1,682	1,581	51.6
1954	652	312	964	855	1,680	1,583	50.9
1955	590	325	915	810	1,775	1,664	45.6
1956	591	352	943	830	1,855	1,741	44.7
1957	614	375	989	869	1,909	1,802	45.5
1958	732	390	1,122	990	1,924	1,832	51.5
1959	627	430	1,057	930	2,003	1,911	46.4

[a]Includes returns from farming operations to resident farm operators for their capital, labor, and management, after deduction of farm production expenses (there is no allowance in the item farm production expenses for a return on investment in farm capital). Also includes farm wages and other farm labor income received by hired farm resident workers.

[b]Includes all income received by farm residents from nonfarm sources such as wages and salaries from nonfarm employment, nonfarm business and professional income, rents from nonfarm real estate, dividends, interest, royalties, unemployment compensation, and social security payments.

TABLE US-7 (Continued)

Per Capita Personal and Disposable Personal Income of U.S. Farm and Nonfarm Populations, 1934-83

YEAR	PER CAPITA PERSONAL INCOME OF FARM POPULATION			PER CAPITA DISPOSABLE PERSONAL INCOME			FARM AS PERCENTAGE OF NONFARM PER CAPITA DISPOSABLE INCOME, ALL SOURCES
	FROM FARM SOURCES[a]	FROM NONFARM SOURCES[b]	FROM ALL SOURCES	OF FARM POPULATION FROM ALL SOURCES	OF NONFARM POPULATION FROM ALL SOURCES	OF TOTAL POPULATION FROM ALL SOURCES	
	(U.S. dollars)						(percent)
1960	711	463	1,174	1,026	2,034	1,947	50.4
1961	771	516	1,287	1,125	2,066	1,991	54.5
1962	796	583	1,379	1,201	2,145	2,073	56.0
1963	824	670	1,494	1,300	2,208	2,144	58.9
1964	773	752	1,525	1,345	2,364	2,296	56.9
1965	968	860	1,828	1,606	2,505	2,448	64.1
1966	1,088	966	2,054	1,793	2,664	2,613	67.3
1967	1,022	1,080	2,102	1,826	2,811	2,757	65.0
1968	1,078	1,227	2,305	1,978	3,010	2,956	65.7
1969	1,254	1,352	2,606	2,202	3,202	3,152	68.8
1970	1,333	1,495	2,828	2,421	3,439	3,390	70.4
1971	1,429	1,623	3,052	2,640	3,667	3,620	72.0
1972	1,764	1,851	3,615	3,073	3,898	3,860	78.8
1973	3,054	2,082	5,136	4,401	4,311	4,315	102.1
1974	2,495	2,378	4,873	4,162	4,691	4,667	88.7
1975[c]	2,994	2,611	5,605	4,854	5,083	5,075	95.5
1976	2,582	2,930	5,512	4,735	5,501	5,478	86.1
1977	2,781	3,314	6,095	5,199	5,989	5,965	86.8
1978	3,551	3,761	7,312	6,222	6,634	6,621	93.8
1979	4,256	4,249	8,505	7,196	7,336	7,331	98.1
1980	2,950	4,717	7,667	6,471	8,074	8,032	80.1
1981	4,376	5,156	9,532	8,007	8,906	8,883	89.9
1982	3,354	5,402	8,756	7,390	9,446	9,397	78.2
1983	2,357	5,752	8,109	6,917	10,057	9,979	68.8

[c]Based on the new farm definition beginning with 1975.

Source: *Economic Indicators of the Farm Sector: Income and Balance Sheet Statistics, 1983*, ECIFS 3-2, Economic Research Service, U. S. Department of Agriculture, September 1984.

area devoted to wheat in other exporting countries equal to about half the U.S. reduction.

It can be argued with considerable validity that for the United States to set its loan rates or price supports above market-oriented levels adversely affects farm income. Because of the major role that the United States has in world trade for the grains and cotton, high price supports increase international market prices and thus encourage increased output in other competing areas. This is true not only if the farmers in other countries directly receive higher prices because of the increased international market prices, but also if the higher international market prices lower the governmental costs of market interventions and thus make possible higher intervention prices than would otherwise occur.

However, the primary effects of supply management efforts and price supports that are not market-oriented are upon governmental costs of the farm programs; and not upon the income of U.S. farmers. The available evidence supports the conclusion that over an extended period of time increasing farm prices is not an effective means of increasing the returns to farm labor and management. It is true that higher prices will be reflected in higher land values, though there is no evidence that higher output prices increase the current return on land or the ratio of rent to the value of the land. One consequence of the effect of higher output prices upon the price of land is that when new farmers enter agriculture by purchasing farm land, they gain little or nothing from the higher output prices. They pay the existing owner of the land for most of the anticipated future returns to the land, including those returns due to higher prices resulting from market interventions. Sadly, however, the farmers who have bought farm land after the market interventions have been instituted stand to lose if the market intervention is eliminated. They stand to lose through loss in the value of their most important asset, farm land. It should thus not be a surprise to anyone that it is difficult to eliminate market interventions; while current farmers gain little from such interventions, they may lose a great deal from their elimination.

Two of the striking changes experienced by agriculture in the United States over the past three decades have been the major reduction in the number of farms and farm workers (including the operator and members of his family) and the rapid increase in the importance of non-farm income in the income of farm families. In 1950 there were 5,648,000 farms and 7,160,000 persons employed in agriculture. By 1970 there were but 2,949,000 farms with employment of 3,463,000. The number of farms has continued to decline to 2,300,000 in 1983 but farm employment has declined very little to 3,321,000 in 1984. Thus while the total net income from farming of all farm operator families, adjusted for changes in the price level, was the same in 1979 as in 1955, the inflation-adjusted or real income per family from farming more than doubled—with half as many families sharing the same total. The annual rate of increase in real incomes of farm families from farm operations was 3 percent.

But over the same period of time (from 1955 to 1979), the real incomes of the farm population more than trebled—actually increased to 3.3 times the 1955 level. This substantial improvement occurred even though farm prices received declined 16 percent relative to prices farmers paid. In terms of current prices, governmental expenditures on farm programs were the same in 1955 and 1979; in terms of dollars of the same purchasing power governmental costs of the farm programs were three times greater in 1955 than in 1979.

In the early 1950s non-farm income accounted for about a third of the income of the farm population; by 1960 non-farm income accounted for 40 percent of total income and by the late 1960s farm and non-farm income sources were equally important. For 1980 through 1983 non-farm income of the farm population was more than 60 percent of total income. Data on sources of income of the farm population are given in Table US-7.

TABLE US-8

Net Farm Income and Off-Farm Income of Farm Operator Families

Year	Net Farm Income	Off-Farm Income	Total Income	Net Farm Income as Percent of Total Income
	(million U.S. dollars)			(percent)
1960	11,518	8,482	20,000	57.6
61	11,957	9,163	21,120	56.6
62	12,064	9,904	21,968	54.9
63	11,770	11,020	22,790	51.6
64	10,492	11,637	22,129	47.4
65	12,899	12,727	25,626	50.3
66	13,960	13,882	27,842	50.1
67	12,339	14,095	26,834	46.0
68	12,322	15,466	27,788	44.3
69	14,293	16,612	30,905	46.2
1970	14,381	17,617	31,998	44.9
71	15,043	19,110	34,153	44.0
72	19,507	21,265	40,772	47.8
73	34,435	24,714	59,149	58.2
74	27,309	28,135	55,444	49.3
75	25,555	23,901	49,456	51.7
76	20,132	26,681	46,813	43.0
77	19,821	26,120	45,941	43.1
78	27,651	29,704	57,355	48.2
79	32,251	35,267	67,518	47.8
1980	21,505	37,660	59,165	36.3
81	30,057	39,877	69,935	43.0
82	22,051	39,431	61,482	35.9
83	16,100	40,933	57,093	28.2

Value of Sales (1982)	Net Farm Income per Farm	Off-Farm Income per Farm	Total Income per Farm	Net Farm Income as Percent of Total Income	Percent of Farms (1982)
	(U.S. dollars)			(percent)	
$500,000 and over	571,097	26,831	597,929	95.5	1.0
$200,000- 499,999	53,461	13,720	67,180	79.6	3.6
$100,000- 199,999	19,786	11,074	30,861	64.1	7.5
$ 40,000- 99,999	5,539	10,615	16,155	34.3	16.1
$ 20,000- 39,999	504	12,887	13,391	3.7	11.4
$ 10,000- 19,999	-728	17,208	16,479	-4.4	11.8
$ 5,000- 9,999	-881	19,146	18,265	-4.8	13.7
$ 2,500- 4,999	-998	19,328	18,330	-5.4	13.6
Less than $ 2,500	-465	20,758	20,292	-2.3	21.4
All Farms	9,959	16,430	26,386	37.7	100.0

Source: *Economic Indicators of the Farm Sector: Income and Balance Sheet Statistics, 1982,* ECIFS 2-2, Economic Research Service, U.S. Department of Agriculture, 1983.

TABLE US-9

**Costs of Farm Price Support and Income Stabilization Programs
to Consumers and Taxpayers in the United States,
1979/80 and 1982/83**

COMMODITY	DOMESTIC USE (A) (million met. ton)	PRICE			VALUE OF DOMESTIC USE AT WORLD PRICES (A×C)	EXCESS CONSUMER COSTS (A×D)
		DOMESTIC (B)	WORLD (C)	DIFFERENCE (B−C=D)		
			($ per metric ton)		($ millions)	
1979/80						
Grains	38.1	140[a]	140[a]	0	5,334	0
Sugar	9.3	552	494	58	4,594	539
Peanuts	1.0	454	438	16	441	16
Tobacco	0.5	3,300	3,300	0	1,650	0
Potatoes	11.6	114	114	0	1,323	0
Poultry	6.2	853	853	0	5,327	0
Eggs	3.6	777	777	0	2,797	0
Pork	7.5	1,382	1,339[b]	43	10,004	322
Beef and veal	10.7	2,508	2,366[b]	142	25,316	1,519
Lamb and mutton	0.15	2,821	2,766[b]	55	415	8
Wool	0.055	4,006	3,530[b]	476	194	26
Butter	0.46	3,154	2,351	803	1,081	369
Nonfat dry milk	0.32	1,966	852	1,114	273	356
Milk, fluid	23.1	286	149	137	3,442	3,165
Milk, mfg.[c]	22.2	259	149	110	3,278	2,442
Cotton lint	1.4	1,372	1,372	0	1,926	0
Vegetable oils	5.3	480	480	0	2,544	0

Value of domestic use at world prices	69,939	
Excess consumer costs		8,406
as percent of value of domestic use at world prices	12%	
Taxpayer costs[d]		3,833
as percent of value of domestic use at world prices	5.4%	
Total costs to consumers and taxpayers		12,239
as percent of value of domestic use at world prices	17.5%	

Note: The estimates of world prices are the actual world prices for the appropriate year. No attempt has been made to reflect what world prices would be if trade were liberalized by the European Community, the United States, Canada and Japan. The important world price changes would be for sugar and dairy products. Domestic use includes only direct human consumption; it does not include grain fed to animals, for instance.

[a]The price of wheat is used for all grains.

[b]The world price is estimated from the U.S. price by assuming that the tariff rates were fully effective. The tariff rates were: beef and veal, 6%; pork, 3.2%; lamb and mutton, 2%; and wool, 13.5%.

[c]Excludes the milk equivalent of butterfat and nonfat dry milk.

[d]The taxpayer costs should not be interpreted as an accurate measure of the income subsidy to farmers. Some part represented payments to farmers for participation in

TABLE US-9 (Continued)

**Costs of Farm Price Support and Income Stabilization Programs
to Consumers and Taxpayers in the United States,
1979/80 and 1982/83**

COMMODITY	DOMESTIC USE (A) (million met. ton)	PRICE			VALUE OF DOMESTIC USE AT WORLD PRICES (A×C)	EXCESS CONSUMER COSTS (A×D)
		DOMESTIC (B)	WORLD (C)	DIFFERENCE (B−C=D)		
		($ per metric ton)			($ millions)	
			1982/83			
Grains	44.4	131[a]	131[a]	0	5,823	0
Sugar	8.1	480	174	306	1,409	2,479
Peanuts	1.2	549	340	209	408	251
Tobacco	0.47	3,892	3,892	0	1,825	0
Potatoes	14.7	108	108	0	1,590	0
Poultry	6.9	865	865	0	5,931	0
Eggs	3.6	752	752	0	2,697	0
Pork	6.8	1,879	1,821[b]	58	12,358	395
Beef and veal	11.4	2,193	2,069[b]	124	23,628	1,418
Lamb and mutton	0.18	2,321	2,276[b]	45	403	8
Wool	0.06	2,747	2,420[b]	327	148	20
Butter	0.4	3,351	2,000	1,351	804	543
Nonfat dry milk	0.2	2,072	847	1,225	181	261
Milk, fluid	18,454	303	127	175	2,349	3,236
Milk, mfg.[c]	25,972	279	104	175	2,694	4,555
Cotton lint	1.2	1,320	1,320	0	1,630	0
Vegetable oils	5.7	454	454	0	2,588	0

Value of domestic use at world prices	66,466	
Excess consumer costs		13,166
as percent of value of domestic use at world prices	19.8%	
Taxpayer costs[d]		19,220[e]
as percent of value of domestic use at world prices	28.9%	
Total costs to consumers and taxpayers		32,386
as percent of value of domestic use at world prices	48.7%	

supply management programs. However, the cost to the taxpayer is real and the dollar amount reflects potential savings that might be achieved under alternative farm and trade policies. The taxpayer costs of nutrition programs, such as food stamps and school lunches, are not included since these programs have nil effects upon farm prices and incomes.

[e]This figure does not include the estimated value of farm commodities given to farmers in 1982/83 for their participation in the Payment-in-Kind (PIK) program. If these commodities are valued at the loan rate, the cost was $9.5 billion. If added to the cash costs, taxpayer costs for 1982/83 were $28.7 billion or about 43 percent of output value at world prices; total consumer and taxpayer costs were $41.9 billion and about 63 percent of output value.

D. Gale Johnson wishes to express appreciation to Barbara J. Mace for her careful preparation of this table.

The last column in Table US-7 shows the substantial improvement in relative income achieved by farm families since the 1950s. During the 1950s the disposable income of the farm population was approximately half that of the non-farm population, on a per capita basis. By 1970, even though relative farm prices declined, the farm income position had improved to 70 percent of the non-farm income. During the 1980-82 period, the per capita income of the farm population averaged somewhat more than 80 percent of the non-farm population. Had the relative importance of non-farm income for farm families remained the same in 1980-82 as in 1960, the farm income in 1980-82 would have been less than 65 percent of the non-farm per capita income. Farm people have shared in the U.S. economic growth for two main reasons: First, many farm people have given up farming to accept alternative employment in non-farm areas and thus reduce the number of people dependent upon farming for their living and, second, the majority of the people now living on farms rely upon non-farm earnings for part or nearly all of their income. Farm people have become fully integrated into the national economy.

Table US-8 also presents data on the importance of off-farm income to farm operator families; the previous table provided data for the farm population which did not include farm operators who lived in non-farm areas and included hired farm workers who lived on farms. Table US-8 gives data for all farm operators regardless of where they live. These data are available only for 1960 to date. Farm operators' dependence upon off-farm income grew from about 40 percent of total income in 1960 to 65 percent in 1982. The bottom part of Table US-8 indicates that for the majority of farm operators, off-farm income accounted for most or all of net income in 1982. Even on farms with sales of $200,000 to $499,999, off-farm income accounted for more than a fifth of total income.

Consumer and Taxpayer Costs of U.S. Farm Programs

Data were earlier presented on the federal government's expenditures upon farm price supports and income stabilization. But governmental expenditures—taxpayer costs— are only a part of the costs; when prices are increased as a result of farm price support programs, citizens in their roles as consumers incur costs. The higher prices that con- sumers must pay for farm products as a result of the price support operations are as real as are the taxpayer costs incurred by the government.

Approximate estimates of the excess costs imposed upon consumers are presented in Table US-9 for 1979/80 and 1982/83; these costs are added to the governmental expendi- tures to arrive at a total for consumer and taxpayer costs. True, these estimates must be interpreted with caution. Consumer costs are estimated by comparing U.S. prices with international market prices. As has been noted, the market interventions by most governents have resulted in the international market prices of most farm products being lower than they would be if all or most governments followed market-oriented farm programs with limited degrees of protection for domestic agriculture. For the majority of farm products, studies indicate that the international market prices have been reduced by national policies by no more than 10 to 15 percent; but there are at least two important exceptions: The international prices of dairy products and sugar have been and are depressed by far more than 10 to 15 percent; the distortions may well be of the order of 50 to 75 percent. Thus the consumer cost estimates should be interpreted with caution. The same degree of caution, of course, should apply in comparing governmental costs since the magnitudes of these costs are influenced by how much international market prices are depressed, in part as a result of the farm programs whose costs we are attempting to estimate.

Consumer and taxpayer costs of the U.S. price support and stabilization programs are given in Table US-9 for 1979/80 and 1982/83. The 1982/83 taxpayer costs—about $19 billion—are distorted to some degree by the very expensive supply management program (PIK) that was in effect in 1983, which was not repeated in 1984 or 1985 and is unlikely to be resorted to in the near future.

For 1979/80 excess consumer costs were estimated to be $8.4 billion or about 12 percent of the estimated value of farm products at international market prices. Taxpayer costs equaled 5.4 percent of domestic use of farm products valued at world market prices. Most of the consumer costs were associated with dairy, beef and sugar.

Excess consumer costs increased sharply by 1982/83 due to increased protection for dairy products and sugar. The increased protection was not due to higher prices in the United States but to much lower international market prices for sugar and manufactured milk products other than butter. In 1982/83 excess consumer costs were estimated at almost 20 percent. Taxpayer costs increased by even more than consumer costs to almost 29 percent of the value of domestic use at international prices. The total of consumer and taxpayer costs amounted to 48.7 percent of the value of domestic use at world prices. The consumer and taxpayer costs are large compared to the net farm incomes of farm operators plus the wages of farm workers. The average for 1979 and 1980 was $41.6 billion; for 1982 and 1983 the average annual total for farm operator income and farm wages was $31.1 billion. Thus in the 1982/83 year the total costs to consumers and taxpayers were slightly larger than the net income from farming for farm operators and hired farm workers.

Who Benefits?
A study undertaken by the U.S. Department of Agriculture provides estimates of the beneficiaries of price support and supply management programs for 1978. The benefits were of two kinds — the actual payments made to farmers and the enhancement of farm prices. Benefits were estimated on a net basis, deducting the amount of income that was foregone on the idled land. The estimated net increase in 1978 farm income was $1.5 billion; the governmental cost of the program was $3.6 billion.

The study estimated that the largest 10 percent of the farms received 55.5 percent of the net benefits; the smallest 70 percent received just 8 percent. The largest 10 percent of the farms that participated in the programs received average payments of $12,000 plus $6,000 in price benefits and gave up about $5,000 in foregone income. The smallest 50 percent of the farms received a net cash gain of about $460 per farm or about a thirtieth of what the largest 10 percent of the farms received. The benefits, as measured, did not accrue wholly to farm operators; a significant fraction went to landlords.

In 1983 when direct payments to farmers were $9.4 billion, $4.1 billion went to farms with sales of $100,000 or more. These farms were 12 percent of the number of farms and received 44 percent of direct payments. The 72 percent of the farmers with the lowest level of sales received 22 percent of the direct payments. The largest 12 percent of the farms had net incomes from farming (before inventory adjustment) of $97,000. These families also had off-farm income averaging $14,000. Their direct governmental payments averaged somewhat more than $14,000.

B. CANADA'S AGRICULTURAL
AND FOOD TRADE POLICIES[1]

A Profile of Canadian Farming
Although only 13 percent of Canada's land area can support agriculture of any kind, its 163 million acres of cultivable land means that it is resource-rich relative to its population of 25 million and has an enviable farm structure. Cultivable area per head of total and farm populations are 6.7 and 339 acres respectively, and average farm size is 511 acres total and 358 acres improved land. There were 318,000 census farms in 1981 (any holding with farm product sales of $250 or more), employing 484,000 people. Of these, 245,000 were operators, 88,000 unpaid family workers and 151,000 paid employees. Total employment in farm production was 4.4 percent of the national labor force and approximately one third of the total number employed in the agri-food sector as a whole. Agricultural production contributed 3.7 percent of gross national product in 1981. However, the picture differs greatly between regions; agricultural value added is about 25 percent of Saskatchewan's provincial product but less than 1 percent of Newfoundland's.

Family-owned and operated businesses are the predominant form of production unit in Canadian agriculture. In 1981, 86.6 percent of farms were individual unincorporated businesses, 9.3 percent were partnerships (mostly of family members), 3.4 percent were family corporations, 0.4 percent were corporate enterprises of other kinds, and 0.3 percent were institutions. Non-family corporations produced only 3.5 percent of aggregate farm output in 1981. Furthermore, as Table CN-1 shows, 82 percent of farm output in 1981 originated on the 97 percent of farms that hired less than two man-years of labor. In terms of tenure, farm operators own about 70 percent of the land they farm and lease about 30 percent. Only 7 percent of the land is farmed by pure tenants, but 55 percent of the land is farmed by part-owners part-tenants, with the owned portion of the land they farm also being about 55 percent.

Examination of the commodity composition of Canadian farm output shows that 86 percent of farm cash receipts in 1983 came from the sale of grains, oilseeds, red meats, milk, eggs and poultry. However, it will be noted that the picture varies greatly between provinces with the dependence of the Prairie provinces on grains and of Central Canada on dairy products having particular policy significance. Regional specialization is paralleled by farm specialization; 95 percent of the farms in Canada that had sales of more than $2,500 in 1981 obtained 50 percent or more of their sales from a single product.

Structural change in agriculture has been continuous but not massive. Thus, the number of census farms fell by 13 percent between 1971 and 1981 and the average size of farms measured in acres increased by 21 percent. Total employment in farming fell by 6 percent in the decade but recently has been stable, though with family workers declining and hired workers providing a higher proportion of the total work force.

These aggregate data mask four crucially important features of Canadian agriculture. First, commercial agriculture is a capital, technology and management intensive *industrialized* activity. Average capital employed in 1981 was $268,000 per worker and $409,000 per farm. This is for all persons employed (including part-time farmers) and all census farms. On commercial farms with sales of more than $70,000, average total assets were just under $1,000,000 in 1981. The amount of capital invested per dollar of value added is eight times higher in agriculture than in Canadian manufacturing as a whole. Further,

---

[1]This essay, except for Table CN-2, is taken from a longer background paper prepared for this project by Prof. T.K. Warley entitled "Canada's Agricultural and Food Trade Policies: A Synoptic View" (1 February 1985).

farmers buy their production inputs from input supply industries with the aid of borrowed operating capital, and sell raw products to a specialized food manufacturing and distribution system which adds two dollars of value for every one contributed in farm production. Purchased inputs and interest payments on borrowed capital now absorb close to two thirds of farm receipts, with interest payments alone absorbing 12 percent of receipts and being the largest single expense of Canada's farmers.

The second characteristic follows: farming in Canada is thoroughly *integrated* into the larger Canadian economy. This means that the performance of the industry and the economic situation of its participants are as much influenced by macro-variables such as growth, interest and inflation rates and by macro-policies such as monetary, fiscal, energy and transport policies as by weather, the state of commodity markets and public agricultural policies *per se*. Canadians who operate farms are also integrated into the wider economy by their great dependence on earnings from off-farm employment, as treated more fully below.

Third, with some 35 to 40 percent of agricultural output being exported, and with relatively low border protection for all commodities save milk and "feather" products, farming in Canada is *internationalized* and integrated into the world food economy. This implies that the situation and outlook for Canadian agriculture depends fundamentally on the evolution of world demand and supply and competitive conditions for agricultural commodities. Additionally, coping with the cyclical and sporadic instabilities transmitted from continental and off-shore markets constitutes an important component of the agricultural policy agenda in Canada.

TABLE CN-1

**Distribution of Farms and Gross Farm Sales by
Organizational Categories, Canada, 1971 and 1981**

FARM STRUCTURAL CATEGORIES	PERCENT OF TOTAL CANADIAN FARMS		PERCENT OF GROSS FARM SALES	
	1971	1981	1971	1981
Larger-than-Family Farms (hire 2 person-years of farm labor)	1.4	2.6	14.5	17.9
Large Family Farms (hire 1-2 person-years of farm labor)	4.0	5.4	12.3	13.6
Full-Time Family Farms (hire 1 person-year of farm labor)	78.1	71.1	68.5	63.4
Small Part-Time Farms (no hired labor; operator works 97 days off farm)	16.6	20.4	4.8	5.1
Totals	100.0	100.0	100.0	100.0

Source: P. Ehrensaft, P. Lamee, R.D. Bollman and F.H. Buttel, "The Microdynamics of Farm Structural Change in North America: The Canadian Experience and Canada-USA Comparisons," invited paper, American Agricultural Economics Association annual meeting, Ithaca, August 1984.

Fourthly, it is important to emphasize that farming in Canada has a very *heterogeneous structure*. In 1981, one percent of Canada's farms produced 19 percent of output as measured by gross farm sales, the top 5 percent accounted for 38 percent of sales and the top quarter 74 percent. Conversely half Canada's census farms are small operations which together produced only 7 percent of aggregate output. This pattern of concentration is also found in commodity subsectors, with dairy, wheat and tobacco farms being notable exceptions. It is apparent that a numerical majority of Canada's census farms are small holdings operated by retirees, hobbyists and multiple-job holders, with farming not being the sole—or even a major—source of income to their occupants.

The heterogeneous structure of farm businesses has important implications for the final attribute of Canada's farming industry to be treated in this section—the economic status of Canada's farmers. Off-farm income is the largest single source of earnings of Canadians who report income from farming, and an important source for those who might be described as commercial farmers insofar as their net farm income is greater than their non-farm income. Indeed, on average in 1980 it was only when gross farm sales reached $7,600 that net farm income was positive and only when farms reached $50,000 of gross sales that net farm income became larger than off-farm income.

The fact that Canadians who farm have multiple sources of income complicates the task of making statements about the social adequacy of the income of farm families and the rates of return to the resources that these families commit to farming activities.

Table 3 in Chapter III of the foregoing report indicates that average incomes of farm families were lower than those of all families prior to the mid-1970s but that since then farm family incomes have been somewhat higher. A 1984 survey by the Farm Credit Corporation showed that the average farm operator had a net worth in his farm business of $420,000, which is thought to be considerably higher than the average wealth of non-farm families.

Despite the focus of agricultural policy on farm income issues, remarkably little is known about the rate of return to resources in Canadian agriculture. The most detailed study which has been done on the matter reported rough parity of returns in farming compared with earnings in other small businesses or with the returns that could have been earned by farmers had they received the wages of non-farm wage earners and invested their capital in common stocks (Brinkman and Gellner, 1977). Larger farms, those with average yearly sales over $50,000 in 1971-74, earned more than parity even if capital gains were excluded. In the latter part of the 1970s farm resource returns improved absolutely and probably relatively. Lower farm incomes and falling land values in the 1981-83 period unquestionably have caused the real rates of return to operator-provided resources in Canadian agriculture to fall. However, it is not known whether returns in agriculture have fallen below the return to comparable resources in other occupations which have also experienced reduced returns and falling asset values as a result of weak markets and escalating costs.

It should be noted that this encouraging sketch of the social adequacy of Canadian farm family incomes and (with much less certainty) of the parity of rates of return to farmer-provided resources on commercial farms, emerges only after very substantial income transfers have been made to farmers by public policies, as discussed below.

About one other aspect of farm incomes in Canada there is no doubt. Incomes of farm operators from farming operations and total farm family incomes are very unstable. They are more unstable than those of other businesses (Brinkman, 1981) and the degree of their variability increased during the 1970s. As will be seen, this characteristic provides a principal motivation for public agricultural policies in Canada.

Selected data for Canadian agriculture over the past two decades are brought together in Table CN-2 in a manner similar to other tables in this appendix for the United States, the European Community and Japan. In contrast to the Community and Japan, but like the United States, Canada is a net exporter of agricultural products—by a wide margin. Agricultural exports and imports were valued at $9.5 billion and $5.2 billion respectively in 1983, representing 11 and 7 percent of total merchandise exports and imports. Exports of grains and oilseeds and their products accounted for 73 percent of total 1983 agri-food exports, with wheat and wheat flour alone generating 50 percent of all receipts from food and agricultural exports. There were also significant positive trade balances in live animals, red meats and tobacco which reflect comparative advantage. The positive trade balance in dairy products by contrast is due to the subsidized production, import restriction and export dumping of manufactured dairy products. Canada's share in world agricultural exports was only 4.3 percent in 1982. However, it has a significant position in world wheat, barley and rapeseed markets, accounting in 1982 for 19.6, 24.6 and 44.3 percent of total world exports of these products respectively. Canada's five leading export markets in 1982 were the United States (25% of exports), the USSR (17%), the EC-9 and Japan (13% each) and China (7%).

Canada accounted for 1.8 percent of world agricultural and food imports in 1982 and, in global terms, was significant only as an importer of sugar (2.5 percent of the world total). About half of all imports are of complementary products. Of the competitive imports, fruits and vegetables are the most important, accounting for 36 percent of all agricultural imports in 1983. The United States is by far the largest single supplier of food and agricultural products (57% of imports in 1982).

The above data emphasize the importance to Canada of an open and well-functioning international market for farm and food products. The surplus on agricultural trade—which represented fully 90 percent of the total national balance on merchandise trade over the period 1970-1981, 25 percent in 1982 and 33 percent in 1983—contributes importantly to the country's balance of payments and to the value of the Canadian dollar. And

TABLE CN-2

Selected Data for Canadian Agriculture, 1962, 1973 and 1983

	1962	1973	1983
Agriculture's share in GDP (%)[a]	5.9	4.6	3.7
Agricultural area (million ha.)[a]	70[d]	69[e]	70
Persons employed (x 1000)[b,c]	653	469	513
Number of farms (x 1000)[b]	481[d]	366[e]	318[f]
Average hectares per farm[b]	145[d]	188[e]	207[f]
Average production per milk cow (kg/head)[b,c]	2,838	3,618	4,210
Average production of wheat (100 kg/ha.)[b]	14.2	16.9	19.6
Average production of all grain (100 kg/ha.)[b]	na	19.3	22.3
External trade: exports ($ Can. billion)[a,b]	1.4	3.0	9.5
External trade: imports ($ Can. billion)[a,b]	0.86	2.2	5.2

[a]Taken from World Bank, *World Tables*.

[b]Taken from Statistics Canada, *Canada Yearbook*.

[c]Taken from Agriculture Canada, *Selected Agricultural Statistics for Canada and the Provinces*.

[d]1961   [e]1971   [f]1981

with the value of agricultural exports being numerically equivalent to 50 percent of gross farm receipts, present and future farmers' incomes and asset values are crucially dependent upon the maintenance and improvement of access to world food markets and successful competition in them.

Public Policies Affecting
Agricultural Output, Consumption, and Trade

Background
Statements on the general orientation of agricultural policies and programs in Canada normally represent them as a subset of national economic policies that are concerned with the attainment of such broad economic and social goals as economic growth and industrial development, increased employment, internal price stability, external payments balance, balanced regional economic development, equitable income distribution and harmonious international relationships (Agriculture Canada, 1977). Increasingly, public policy is couched in terms of the whole agri-food system, with emphasis on the role of government in promoting development by the provision of public goods and correcting for market failures (Agriculture Canada, 1981; Whelan, 1983). In this sense, public agri-food policy is represented as "food policy" and as a development-oriented, productivity-enhancing and competitiveness-promoting "sector-specific industrial strategy".

A good number of the programs that federal and provincial Departments of Agriculture administer are consistent with this thrust and the positive purpose:

> to develop and expand Canada's production and export strengths, to ensure the adequacy of safe and nutritious food supplies for the domestic and export markets at reasonable prices which are responsive to competitive forces over time (Whelan and Abbot, 1977).

Programs concerned with research and extension, market information, product and market development, protecting the resource base, food safety, plant and animal health, competition policy, international commercial diplomacy, etc., are all of this type. Such programs enhance welfare for all groups; they are not controversial within the country and their external trade effects are negligible or incidental.

Research, development and extension for the food system are publicly funded in Canada as elsewhere. Annual expenditures were a little over $400 million in 1983/84. Such expenditures no doubt have a very significant effect over the long run on Canadian agricultural output and thereby on trade, but in international trade policy terms they are generally not regarded as conferring an unfair competitive advantage.

Alongside the developmental/public goods themes of agri-food strategy are others with protectionist, preservationist and adjustment-ameliorating flavors and results. These constitute the stuff of traditional "farm" policy. Programs of this nature usually entail the transfer of income to farmers though they are normally represented as being concerned with the objectives of preserving the family farm, enhancing farm income stability and equity and ensuring its adequacy, and import substitution and export expansion. Programs with these intents are directed at the farming component of the food system. Because they do have trade effects such programs are contestable in international fora. They are the major focus of this report.

Before going on, however, it is important to stress that while statements about Canadian agricultural policy objectives include such phrases as "to provide farmers with a standard of living (including monetary rewards, working conditions and public services) comparable to that enjoyed by other Canadians" (Agriculture Canada, 1980), farm policy in Canada—unlike that in the EC for instance—is not conducted against a background of an official or public perception of general income inadequacy among farmers in either a social or economic parity sense. Rather the major official theme is that of protecting the incomes of efficient producers from domestic and international market price instabilities. That is, save for the programs for milk and feather products, the emphasis of commodity policy is on price and income stabilization around market-oriented levels, rather than their support above competitive levels as part of a general commitment to underwrite "remunerative prices" and to provide farmers with "adequate incomes" and "fair returns".

Stabilization policy is justified in terms of promoting allocative efficiency, maintaining viable units in the face of market perturbations by providing economic safety nets, and sharing with farmers the risks of the output-expanding orientation of national food strategy. It will be seen below that the Agricultural Stabilization Act, the Western Grains Stabilization Act, aspects of marketing board programs, and some elements of agricultural trade and farm taxation policy have this stabilization feature. There are also, of course, appeals to notions of distributive justice in the sense that stabilization payments are sometimes represented as having a "compensatory" element.

On the other hand, it will also be seen that if farmer income inadequacy has not recently been a rhetorical theme of Canadian agricultural policy, this is due in large measure to the fact that approximate social and economic parity for agriculture has been achieved by massive transfers of income to Canada's farmers from Canadian taxpayers and consumers and from producers in other countries. The commodity policies for milk, eggs and poultry meats explicitly guarantee their producers remunerative returns, and transport subsidies and tariffs bolster the incomes of grain growers and fruit and vegetable producers respectively directly and significantly. Credit subsidies and taxation expenditures also enhance the income of Canadian farmers as a whole, though their impacts are not commodity specific.

Five other generic features of Canadian agricultural policy may be noted. First, responsibility for agricultural policy and programs is divided between federal and provincial levels of government. Recently divisions of responsibility have become less clear. Provinces have become involved in price and income support and credit programs, crop insurance is a shared program, and federal and provincial governments are partners in national pricing, marketing and trade arrangements for industrial milk, eggs and poultry. This has important implications for the ability of the federal government to meet commitments it might make in international negotiations on agricultural production and trade.

Second, agricultural policy in Canada evolves incrementally by program and over time. There is no parallel to the annual review and determination of policy conducted by the EC's Council of Ministers or to the omnibus farm legislation enacted at four year intervals in the United States.

Third, in a paper focused on the trade effects of national farm programs, it is worth observing that federal agricultural policy in Canada has no targets for the proportions of the consumption of all food or of specific commodities that should be met from indigenous sources. Industrial milk is an exception in that policy is geared to self-sufficiency in butterfat. And, of course, mercantilist attitudes on the desirability of export expansion and the imperatives of import substitution flourish in Canada, as elsewhere.

Fourth, it can be observed that in recent years the trajectory of government intervention in agriculture has been upwards. This is manifest in the progressive enrichment and proliferation of federal and provincial commodity stabilization programs, completion of the national formula pricing/supply management programs for feather products, proposals for the introduction of supply management programs for red meats and potatoes and their extension for tobacco, the granting of increased tariff protection for producers and processors of some fruits and vegetables, and the provision to farmers of rising benefits under transportation, credit and taxation programs. This escalation of support for Canadian agriculture is attributable in part to an interventionist mood in government, partly to a wish to insulate the domestic food system from external shocks, and partly to a desire to relieve agriculture from the stress and difficulties associated with market and cost instabilities and to share with farmers the risks of the development-oriented food strategy that has been judged to be in the broad national interest (Agriculture Canada, 1981).

Finally it may be noted here that the large income transfers which are being made to Canadian farmers by policy in three areas (milk, feather products and transport subsidies, see below) were in large measure quite unplanned. Thus, it is doubtful if any politician or public official anticipated that the policy for industrial milk formally introduced in 1975 would be costing consumers and taxpayers well over half a billion dollars a year a decade later. It is certain that no one anticipated that the 4,000 registered producers of eggs and poultry meats would be permitted by inadequate regulation to use their monopoly powers to transfer to themselves around $100 million a year from Canadian consumers and to pump up the aggregate value of their quota rights to well over $1 billion. And the enormous transfers implicit in the Crow's Nest Pass statutory freight rates for Western grains only developed in the 1970s as rail haulage costs escalated.

General Policy Measures

The special provisions made for agriculture in the fields of monetary (interest rate), fiscal (taxation), transport and trade policy all directly influence the position of Canadian producers in the international marketplace and as such might be the subject of discussion in international fora dealing with agricultural trade issues.

Credit. Monetary policy affects agriculture through the general level of interest rates as well as through the exchange rate. Farmers now borrow the major part of the capital they use from commercial credit institutions at competitive interest rates. However, significant proportions of the long term mortgage capital, of the medium term funds used for farm improvements, and, more recently, of the loans made to farm businesses in financial difficulties are provided by federal and provincial credit agencies at concessional interest rates. No estimate of the total income transfer to farmers through credit subsidies is available, nor of their impact on the level, location and composition of farm output. However, it could be significant, particularly in some provinces and for some products where extensive credit subsidies are provided.

Taxation. Like farmers in other countries, Canadian farmers benefit through numerous special provisions and derogations in the taxation code. These include tax concessions and investment incentives. The former embrace such measures as rebates on property taxes; cash accounting, livestock inventory valuation and income averaging privileges; and the deferral of taxes on capital gains on within-family farm transfers. Again, no estimate exists of the value to farmers of these tax expenditures, but they are thought to be very large indeed. Their overall effects on incentives and investment would be correspondingly significant. But little can be said other than that, to the extent they encourage output expansion, they are not trade-neutral.

Transport. Transport policy is an important component of Canadian economic and regional development policy and the level, location, composition and international competitiveness of Canadian agricultural output has been rather directly affected by elements of it.

By far the most important are the effects of statutory (Crow's Nest Pass) freight rates on the movement by rail of grains and oilseeds from the Prairies to export positions and the funding from the public purse of investments in railway infrastructure, hopper-cars and grain handling and storage facilities. As costs increased in the 1970s, fixed freight rates involved very large income transfers to prairie grain growers who received higher net prices than they would have obtained if paying competitive freight rates. In general, the transport subsidies provided incentives to increase the production in the West of grains and oilseeds for export (or their processing and feeding in Eastern Canada) whilst discouraging the development of animal agriculture and agricultural processing in Western Canada. However, the grain production and export incentive has been offset to an unknown degree by mounting constraints on delivery capacity as the grain transportation system deteriorated with disinvestment. Under recent legislation (Western Grain Transportation Act, 1983), the federal government will pay the 1981/82 "Crow Gap" of $659 million in perpetuity (plus a falling share of subsequent freight cost increases) and also continue for a time to make substantial investments in the modernization of railway infrastructure and the equipment fleet. Furthermore, if the freight subsidy continues to be paid to the railways rather than to producers after the 1985/86 crop year, the incentive to the production and export of the grains, oilseeds and specialty crops that benefit from the statutory rate system will remain.

There are other transport and transport-related subsidies affecting Canadian agriculture—e.g., the Feed Freight Assistance program, the Maritime Freight Rate, the Atlantic Freight Assistance Acts and assistance to the building of grain elevators and terminal facilities—but none of these are nearly as significant as the statutory grain freight rates from a trade policy perspective.

Trade Arrangements. Within the general framework of Canadian trade policy, some provisions for agricultural products are designed to achieve the income, stability, output and employment goals of farm and food policy.

On the export side, agricultural exports are aided by various foreign market identification and assistance schemes and institutional arrangements. These include state-trading agencies—Canadian Wheat Board (CWB) and Canadian Dairy Commission (CDC)—and various export financing, insurance and guarantee arrangements. Direct export subsidies are available in the form of concessional credit but are used very sparingly. Output of regulated products surplus to domestic requirements at administered internal prices is dumped on world markets for whatever price it will fetch. This is a persistent practice with skimmed milk powder and evaporated milk, and occurs sporadically with eggs. Regular annual shipments of some 600,000 tonnes of grains as food aid are also of benefit to producers, as are occasional donations of other products. Bilateral trade arrangements give some stability, predictability and preference in the volume of grain exports to the centrally planned economies, but they have no price provisions.

On the import side, general trade legislation provides "conditional protection" in the form of anti-dumping, countervail and temporary safeguards measures which from time to time have been applied to imports of unfairly priced or intolerably disruptive agricultural and food products. These have to meet an injury test and use transparent procedures, and they are fully in conformity with the GATT.

Ostensibly, so too are the restrictive licensing and quantitative limits placed on imports of competitive products. These apply to imports of manufactured dairy products, eggs and poultry meats and are designed to defend the support prices established under national supply control programs.

Beef and veal imports are also subject to licensing and quantitative restrictions and these are unaccompanied by national supply control. However, the aggregate beef and veal quota is set at a non-restrictive level and is governed by an automatically rising minimum access commitment. Hence, the Meat Import Law is best regarded as a safeguard measure rather than a protective arrangement.

With some exceptions, the tariff is not an important protective instrument for Canadian agriculture. Many agricultural products enter duty free, other tariffs have been bound and reduced in successive rounds of GATT negotiations. The United States and Canada have gone a long way to bind, harmonize and reduce tariffs and remove tariff quotas on agricultural products that are traded mainly in the continental market. The most significant preferential tariff that remains is the one cent a pound duty that favors imports of sugar from Australia.

The tariff is the principal instrument used to support the Canadian horticultural industry. Tariff calendars prevail for many fruits and vegetables, and for some of these the tariffs were increased in 1979. Tariffs also provide significant effective protection to tobacco growers and to a number of agricultural processing and food manufacturing activities.

Imports of farm and food products into Canada are also impeded—though not necessarily with a protective intent—by a host of non-tariff barriers. These include packaging and labelling requirements, valuation and documentation procedures and health and phyto-sanitary regulations. Interestingly, as Canada's livestock populations, plant materials and food supply become increasingly "clean," the growing risks and costs of contamination are resulting in Canada's regulations becoming more restrictive over time. This in itself is posing a growing obstacle to the attainment of a more open trading system—particularly in live animals and livestock products—and an increasingly important source of conflict with trading partners.

Commodity Policies

A brief account is given in this section of the more important commodity-oriented programs used to give price and income support to Canadian agriculture.

Agriculture Stabilization Act 1975 (ASA). This program provides *(ex post)* floor prices to producers. Deficiency payments are made following periods of low prices. (Occasionally, when rapid intervention is required, support purchases are made under the Agricultural Products Board Act instead.) The minimum support price for each of nine named commodities (beef cattle, hogs, sheep and lambs, industrial milk and cream, corn, soybeans, and oats and barley grown outside the designated area of the CWB) is set at not less than 90 percent of the average market price over the previous five years, adjusted by the difference between production costs per unit in the current year and average unit production costs in the previous five year reference period. The minimum floor price for the named commodities may be more than 90 percent of the average market price of the previous five years. Other products may be designated from time to time (e.g., potatoes, soft wheat, sugar beet, grapes, tree fruits) and for these the floor price may be less than 90 percent of the previous five year average. Provincial governments and producers do not contribute to expenditures on this program. A proposed national, voluntary, tripartite, cost-shared stabilization plan for red meats could provide more benefits to producers than has resulted from the ASA (Agriculture Canada, 1984).

Payments under the ASA to producers of products other than industrial milk and cream have been sporadic and variable. Federal government payments on such products were $138 million in 1981/82 but fell to $6 million in 1982/3. They averaged $49 million annually in the period 1974/5 to 1982/3. Purchases by the Agricultural Products Board have usually cost less than $10 million a year. To avoid trade conflicts, payments are made only on production consumed domestically.

Provincial Stabilization Programs. The federal ASA (except for payments to producers of industrial milk and cream) has been steadfastly market-oriented, stop-loss and stabilizing in intent and designed to be resource and market neutral. Producers and provincial governments have judged its benefits to be too modest. Its operation has also been deficient insofar as the data base on returns and costs is inadequate, floor prices are not known in advance, and payments are uncertain (and to some degree discretionary) and are made too late to prevent farm businesses succumbing in periods of sharp cost increases and weak product prices (Agriculture Canada, 1984). Accordingly, all provincial governments except Newfoundland have introduced a wide variety of ad hoc support payments or ongoing commodity stabilization or "assurance" programs for producers in their jurisdictions. The provisions of these provincial programs vary greatly by commodity and by province, in the extent of producer contributions to stabilization funds, and in the levels of product price guarantees to producers. In the most generous schemes producers are guaranteed full-cost determined support prices. Expenditures on provincial stabilization programs averaged $74 million annually between 1974/5 and 1982/3, i.e., 50 percent more than federal expenditures under the ASA on non-dairy commodities in the same period.

The "top-loading" of the federal ASA by provincial programs is distorting regional production incentives in Canada and is a growing problem for Canadians. More importantly for this study, it has the potential to become an important international trade policy issue—particularly with the United States—and one with which the federal government is finding it difficult to deal because of its limited ability to control the agricultural programs of provincial governments. In recent years the federal government has threatened to deduct from its payments under the ASA amounts equal to the sums received by producers from parallel but richer provincial programs. However, in practice, this has not been done consistently.

Western Grain Stabilization. The federal Western Grains Stabilization Act 1976 provides growers of wheat, barley, oats, rye, flaxseed, rapeseed and mustard seed in the designated area of the CWB with an assurance that their aggregate and per tonne net cash flow in the current year will not fall below the average of the previous five years. When the net cash flow (gross receipts minus cash production expenses) for a crop year falls below the five year average, a payment is made equal to the shortfall. It is a voluntary program under which participating producers contribute to a stabilization fund two percent of their gross receipts (currently to a maximum of $60,000). The federal government contributes $2 to the fund for every $1 provided by producers.

Prior to 1984 payments under the WGSA had been infrequent and modest ($115 million in 1977 and $253 million in 1978). Indeed the program had so small an influence on farm income and production stability in Western Canada that its provisions were changed in 1984 to provide producers with larger and more timely benefits in periods of economic stress (Agriculture Canada, 1984). Even so, while public expenditure is involved, the WGSA, like the ASA, will continue to be a stabilization rather than a support program, i.e., it provides a market-determined, low-slung, safety net in low price periods rather than guarantees of remunerative prices and returns determined by producers' costs of production and income needs.

The same can be said of the *initial prices* paid to Western grain producers upon delivery of their crops to elevators. For although these prices are guaranteed for individual grains by the federal government, they are set cautiously and in relation to anticipated world market prices. Federal payments under these guarantees have been rare and small.

Grain storage is not directly subsidized in Canada as it is in the United States. Instead the costs of holding undeliverable grains and commmercial inventories are borne directly by private grain companies and by producers either on their farms or through marketing costs incurred by the CWB.

No one would claim that the *Crow's Nest Pass freight rates system* (outlined earlier) is designed to stabilize the economic environment of prairie agriculture, though it does have incidental stability-enhancing effects. Originally intended as an instrument of economic development for Western Canada, it has been transformed by rapidly rising grain haulage costs into an arrangement whereby huge annual income transfers are made to Western grain producers from Canadian taxpayers, Western livestock producers and processors and railway shareholders.

Likewise the commodity programs sketched below for milk and feather products—whilst they too have stability features—are primarily arrangements that hold the incomes of the producers of these products above competitive levels.

Dairy Industry Support. In policy terms milk pricing and income maintenance programs are divided into arrangements for fluid and industrial milk.

Fluid milk pricing and marketing fall under provincial jurisdiction. In each province, producers' marketing boards with monopsony/monopoly powers (or quasi-governmental regulatory agencies) price fluid milk on the basis of calculated "full" costs of production including the opportunity costs of farmer-provided resources. Aggregate output is then limited by producer quotas to the amount that is demanded at that price. Little milk crosses provincial boundaries and none may be imported from the United States.

Industrial milk policy is basically the responsibility of the federal government though, in practical terms, its administration is a joint operation of the CDC (a federal agency), provincial governments and provincial producers' milk marketing boards. Target prices for manufacturing milk are set administratively in relation to costs of production and negotiated rates of return to the resources producers commit to milk production (a base price is adjusted periodically by reference to an economic index). The target price is implemented by a direct flat rate unit subsidy (which has been constant for some years at $6.03 per hectoliter of 3.6 percent fat milk) and by the support purchasing operations of the CDC. The internal price is defended by quantitative restrictions on the importation of manufactured dairy products and by restrictions on the importation, use and/or properties of dairy product substitutes. Skim milk powder surplus to domestic demand at the CDC's support price is acquired by the CDC and sold abroad. Aggregate milk output is determined by the national amount of butterfat that is demanded at the CDC's support-buying price for butter. Each province and each licensed producer has a marketing quota equal to their share of target national output.

In trade policy terms the salient features are the heavy subsidization of high cost milk production in Canada, the rigid control of imports of competing dairy products and the dumping abroad of skim milk powder. In mitigation it is claimed by government authorities and by milk producers that—unlike the EC and the United States—the response to incentive prices is limited by the supply control program and that this contributes to international market stability. The import controls on fluid milk and manufactured dairy products are in conformity with the legal provisions of the GATT. It is also noted that producers bear the loss on powder exports through a within-quota levy that absorbs most of the direct subsidy. Efficient foreign suppliers might respond that a policy of perpetual self-sufficiency in fresh milk and butterfat achieved by direct and indirect subsidies is not in conformity with the obligation to acknowledge the evolution of international comparative advantage, that the cheese import quota has consciously reduced the share of imports in consumption below historic levels (from 13 percent in 1975 to 9 percent in 1982), and that Canadian taxpayers ultimately pay the cost of subsidizing skim milk powder exports.

Egg and Poultry Support. The arrangements for pricing, production and trade in eggs, chickens and turkeys are broadly the same as those described above for milk. That is, producer prices are determined by economic formulae (nationally for eggs and provincially for poultry) that provide full cost recoupment, aggregate output is limited by quotas to the amount demanded at those prices (with negotiated shares for each province and each licensed producer), and imports are controlled by licensing and import quotas to defend the internal price structure. No direct subsidies are paid by federal or provincial governments; income transfers to producers of the "feather products" are entirely from Canadian consumers. Internal prices are normally much higher than in the United States (and on world markets) and were it not for the border restrictions considerable quantities of imports would be attracted at the current support price. However, the aggregate import quotas were set at historic import shares of the Canadian market (6.3, 2.0 and 1.7 percent of domestic production for broilers, turkeys and eggs respectively) and foreign suppliers share in market growth. Hence the quotas are not trade distorting, and they are, of course, in legal conformity with the requirements of Article XI of the GATT.

Other Commodity Policies. Price and output fixing marketing boards are an integral part of the arrangements discussed above for giving support to Canadian producers of fluid milk, industrial milk, cream, eggs and poultry meats, but all other marketing boards operate within the parameters of continental and world markets (Forbes, Hughes and Warley, 1982). The latter boards do much to correct for market imperfections, expand demand and foster improvements in the operational and pricing efficiency of markets, but they do not have the power to affect producer prices in any non-competitive way. Hence they have no direct effects on production, and thence on trade.

Grape growers and wineries benefit greatly from the discriminatory procurement and margin policies of provincial liquor monopolies, from capital development grants and from sporadic assistance to grape prices given under stabilization programs.

Table CN-3 draws together in summary form the major commodity-specific policy instruments used in Canada affecting output, consumption and trade. It is not possible to identify the incidence on specific commodity production and trade systems of public policies in the areas of subsidized credit, research, extension and inspection services, and taxation expenditures, or from the phyto-sanitary regulations and the miscellany of other non-tariff measures that impede imports (or assist exports) of farm and food products. These are therefore not included in Table CN-3. It should be emphasized, however, that these measures together may have a very large impact on the competitive position of Canadian producers in the Canadian and international markets. Indeed, for all one knows, their combined trade effects may be as large as those of the more visible programs that are identified in the Table.

Overview
It will be apparent that Canadian agriculture as a whole and some specific commodity subsystems are subject to a considerable measure of government intervention and economic regulation both within national borders and at the frontier.

At first blush, some of the stabilization measures (e.g., ASA, WGSA and the less-generous provincial programs) might be regarded as being essentially trade neutral. The pricing, production and trade arrangements for eggs and poultry meats probably have no adverse effects on foreign suppliers and so, while they are of great concern to Canadians, they do not constitute a trade policy issue between Canada and her trading partners.

The major areas of intervention that do have significant and visible trade effects and that raise important trade policy issues are the parameters of Canadian dairy policy, the transport subsidies given to Western grain production and export, the subsidy elements in credit policies and the richer provincial stabilization programs, and the tariffs that accord protection to the horticultural and other industries.

This does not exhaust the list of implicit opportunities for Canada to make constructive contributions to the more efficient use of world agricultural resources and a better-functioning international trading system. For instance, changes might be made in the less transparent ways in which Canada assists its agricultural producers *vis-à-vis* their foreign competitors, e.g., through tax expenditures and technical barriers to trade.

Economic Effects of Intervention in Canadian Agriculture

This section presents a synopsis of the results of the work of others who have studied empirically the level of support given to Canadian agriculture by the policy instruments

TABLE CN-3

Major Commodity Specific Policy Instruments Affecting Output, Consumption and Trade, Canada, 1984

	Wheat	Barley	Corn	Soybeans	Canola Products	Cattle	Hogs	Beef and Veal	Pork	Sheepmeat	Chicken	Turkey	Eggs	Fluid Milk	Industrial Milk	Butter	Cheese	Powdered Milk	Sugar	Potatoes	Fruits and Vegetables	Tobacco	Grapes/Wine
Product Support																							
Price & margin support																							
Full cost pricing											★	★	★	★	★								
Floor pricing	★	★	★	★	★	★	★		★										★	★	★	★	
Margin support	★	★			★																		
Two prices	★																						
Supply control											★	★	★	★	★								★
Trade controls																							
Tariffs	★	★	★					★	★	★	★	★	★	★	★		★	★	★	★	★	★	★
Quotas								★			★	★	★			★	★						
Licensing	★	★						★			★	★	★	★		★	★	★					
State trading	★	★														★		★					★
Export subsidies																		★					
Food aid	★																	★					
Input subsidies																							
Transport	★	★			★																		
Storage																				★	★		
Crop insurance	★	★	★	★	★															★	★	★	★

identified in the previous section, and who have measured the output, consumption and trade effects of this intervention.

Budgetary Expenditures

Budgetary expenditures on agriculture and food in the two most recent fiscal years for which data are available, 1980/81 and 1981/82, are shown in Table CN-4. Expenditures at both federal and provincial levels rose markedly in nominal terms from the mid-1970s but fell in real terms. Currently, total expenditures are equivalent to about 1 percent of GNP, 17 percent of gross farm receipts, 40 percent of value added in agriculture and 66 percent of aggregate net farm income. Price and income support expenditures are about half of

TABLE CN-4

Federal and Provincial Budgetary Expenditures on Agriculture, Canada, Fiscal Years 1980/81 and 1981/82
(millions of Canadian dollars)

	FEDERAL		PROVINCIAL		TOTAL	
	1980/1	1981/2	1980/1	1981/2	1980/1	1981/2
Administrative	172.3	154.5	79.3	88.4	251.6	242.9
Research & Advisory						
Research	88.1	118.7	41.2	44.7	129.3	163.4
Advisory	26.0	29.3	106.7	120.7	132.7	150.0
Inspection, Pest & Disease Control	100.9	112.1	na	na	100.9	112.1
Rationalization						
Rationalization of Production	162.2	98.0	5.5	6.7	167.7	103.5
Structural Reorganization & Improvements	20.1	18.6	97.4	86.0	117.5	104.6
Processing & Marketing	33.9	35.8	350.9	361.6	384.8	397.4
Price & Income Support[1]	954.5	1153.7	275.9	431.0	1230.4	1584.7
Technical and Food Aid	212.0	263.0	—	—	212.0	263.0
Total	1770.8	1983.6	957.9	1139.1	2726.9	3121.6
Expenditures on Price & Income Support						
: as % of gross farm cash receipts[2]	6	6	2	2	2	8
: % of net farm income[2]	30	24	9	9	39	33

[1]Major items include dairy subsidy, stabilization payments, crop insurance and transport and credit subsidies. Implicit railway subsidies to producers and tax expenditures are excluded.

[2]Fiscal 1980/81 and 1981/82 expenditures as a proportion of calendar 1980 and 1981 receipts and incomes.

Source: Data provided by Agriculture Canada.

total expenditures, 8 percent of total farm cash receipts and about one third of the net income of Canada's farmers. Extension and market development have historically taken a large share of provincial expenditures, while the federal government has concentrated on price and income support, research and inspection services. More recently the provinces have spent rising sums on price and income support, including credit subsidies.

Degrees of Protection
While public expenditures on price and income supports represent a large source of the income transfers made to Canadian producers, they are not the whole story. Farmers also gain from market control programs, trade measures, additional transport subsidies and taxation expenditures. However, from these sources of gain must be deducted the effects of the tariffs and taxes and other measures that raise the cost to farmers of intermediate inputs and so reduce value-added in agriculture.

Lattimore (1982) has provided the only estimate available of net rates of effective protection to Canadian agriculture as a whole over an extended period and using a standard methodology. His results are reproduced in Table CN-5. It will be seen that the effective rate of protection to Canadian agriculture has varied a great deal over the years, but in the decade of the 1970s averaged 60 percent when all support (except tax expenditures) is counted (scenario C).

Other authors have calculated measures of protection for commodity sub-sectors in various time periods. There is considerable variation according to the period studied, as would be expected with fluctuating commodity prices and variations in the form, coverage and level of government support. However, protection rates have been low (and occasionally negative) for oilseeds, corn, and pork, while milk and the feather products have consistently had high rates of protection in Canada. Estimates of the effective protection rates for wheat and barley, with one important exception, show modest assistance. Studies by the OECD Secretariat of producer subsidy and consumer tax equivalents by commodities for the period 1977-1981 will also show the dairy and feather segments to be the most highly protected and assisted parts of Canadian agriculture.

Transfers and Efficiency Losses
Agricultural policies transfer very large sums of money between Canadian producers and consumers/taxpayers. Among commodities, the transfers for milk are by far the greatest. According to Barichello's estimates (1982), the total gain to producers for the six commodities he examined was $1,893 million in 1980 (milk accounting for about half), equivalent to 60 percent of aggregate net farm income in that year, or about $7,000 per farm for each of the 270,000 farms with sales over $2,500 per year. The estimated cost to consumers of supporting the incomes of the producers of these products was around $1,127 million and the cost to taxpayers was $819 million (with milk accounting for about two thirds of the combined total). With annual gains to farmers averaging $7,000 each and losses to consumers/taxpayers being less than $80 per head per year, it is not difficult to understand why agricultural policies are so decisively important to producers but of peripheral interest to those who bear their costs. This does much to explain their durability.

Barichello calculates that the economic loss to society as a whole from policy-induced distortions in resource use and consumption for the six products studied was $249 million in 1980. The desire to transfer income to producers is not the only reason for supporting Canadian agriculture, but it is an important one. In this regard, it is worth noting that the national economic loss per dollar of income transferred was 22 cents for

TABLE CN-5

Effective Rate of Producer Protection (ERP)[1], Canadian Agriculture, 1971-80

		1971	1972	1973	1974	1975	1976	1977	1978	1979	1980
		(millions of current Canadian dollars)									
Farm Cash Receipts											
1. domestic prices		4541	5510	6968	9011	10057	10088	10212	12040	14283	15665
2. border prices		4067	5047	6430	8129	8819	8680	8768	10694	12720	13963
Total Purchased Inputs											
3. domestic prices		2594	2852	3464	4305	4921	5578	5922	6917	8159	9336
4. border prices		2501	2705	3274	4073	4661	5368	5702	6643	7823	8956
Farm Value Exports		1598	1723	2147	3164	3230	3231	3410	3815	4798	6302
5. Adjustment		112	121	150	221	226	226	239	267	336	441
Imported Input Cost		455	488	570	704	837	1004	1077	1237	1447	1658
6. Adjustment		32	34	40	49	58	70	75	86	101	116
7. Gov't and Other Input Cost (C)		532	568	588	808	873	961	1324	1063	1100	1270
Value-Added											
8. domestic prices[2]		1947	2658	3504	4706	5136	4510	4290	5123	6124	6329
9. border prices[3]		1114	1861	2678	3420	3453	2507	1906	3169	4032	4062
		(percent)									
ERP[1]	A[4]	29	16	13	21	29	47	70	34	29	30
	B[5]	43	24	18	28	39	64	94	49	44	48
	C[6]	75	43	31	38	49	80	125	62	52	56

[1]ERP equals (VA^d-VA^b) as a percentage of VA^b, where VA is value-added and b and d represent border and domestic prices respectively.

[2]Row 1 less row 3.

[3]Value added adjusted for tariffs, NTBs, direct government program payments and government contributions to crop insurance, producer financing, and government and railway contributions to grain and oilseed transportation, with further adjustments for structural over/under valuations of the exchange rate. Value-added at border prices is row 2 plus row 5 less row 4 less row 6 less row 7.

[4]Scenario A includes only Federal and provincial commodity program expenditures.

[5]B includes expenditures under commodity programs, federal crop insurance, federal producer financing, federal trade promotion and federal contributions to grain transportation.

[6]C as B plus railway contribution to grain transportation (the "Crow Gap"). Scenario C has been used in constructing row 7. Row 8 less row 9 as a percentage of row 9 gives scenario C outcomes.

Source: Lattimore (1982), Table B.5. For further details, readers are referred to Appendix B in Lattimore's paper.

milk, 24 cents for poultry and 35 cents for eggs. Thus, the transfer mechanisms employed for the most heavily subsidized sectors of Canadian agriculture appear to be rather cost ineffective.

This is even more true when they are considered in a long-term perspective, for there is ample evidence that income transfers quickly become capitalized into the value of assets in inelastic supply, enriching their first generation recipients but leaving their successors with higher entry barriers and a permanently raised and dangerously bur-densome cost structure. For instance "the Crow benefit" is usually reckoned to have raised Western grain-land prices by $30 an acre (Harvey, 1980), while Table CN-6 shows the extraordinary value taken on by production and marketing quotas in Canada as a result of the high and stable returns provided to producers under the national formula pricing/supply management programs for milk, eggs and poultry and tobacco.

These and other estimates of the income transfers and national income losses arising from major commodity programs and the significance of quota values have been hotly contested by farmers' organizations (see, for example, Ontario Milk Marketing Board, 1984). However, producer organizations have not yet provided alternative and more credible estimates of the benefits they derive from farm programs. Meanwhile, un-published work by the OECD Secretariat appears to endorse the results found by Canadian and U.S. researchers.

Trade Effects
Lattimore's work led him to an estimate of the aggregate agricultural trade effect of the protection given to Canadian agriculture. As shown in Table CN-7, under all scenarios, the effect of abandoning internal agricultural policies and associated frontier measures that affect production and consumption and thence net export availabilities and net import requirements would have been to greatly reduce Canada's 1980 positive agri-cultural trade balance of $2.6 billion. Even allowing for a terms of trade effect, it is estimated that the net trade balance could have been 40-60 percent lower at $1.6 to $1.0 billion.

Other authors have calculated the export expanding and import reducing effects of Canada's farm and food programs by commodity. Estimates vary amongst the authors, reflecting differences in periods covered, methods and assumptions. It would appear from this work that without support Canada might be exporting each year approximately 1 million tonnes less each of wheat and barley and moving from being a net exporter of

TABLE CN-6

Market Value of Quotas, Ontario, 1984

(Canadian dollars)

Product	Unit Price	Family-Sized Unit	Quota Cost to Enter
Fluid Milk	$200/liter/day		
Mfrg. Milk	$0.90/liter/year	40 cows	$180,000
Eggs	$30/hen	25,000 layers	$750,000
Broilers	$10/unit	50,000 birds/cycle	$450,000
Turkeys	$0.70/lb.	25,000 birds/yr.	$350,000
Tobacco	$2.00/lb.	40 acres	$400,000

almost 10 million hectoliters of milk equivalent (1979-81 average) to a net importer of some 23 million hl per year (in the form of products)—a net trade change of 30.7 million hl or 1.39 mmt milk equivalent. Sugar imports might be some 500,000 tonnes greater, and net beef imports might increase by some 60,000 tonnes or about 5 percent of national consumption. There would be very little change in trade in eggs, poultry meats and (less surely) pork, though for the first two of these commodities, abandoning the formula pricing and supply management arrangements and opening the border would entail a precipitous reduction in producers' incomes and the value of their quotas and other assets.

It must be stressed that the empirical work lying behind such figures produces results that must be taken with extreme caution. This is so for a number of reasons. First, net trade is a residual reflecting disproportionately errors in production and consumption estimates. Second, good information on single commodity supply and demand elasticities is rarely available, especially outside the price ranges provided by policy. More important yet, information on cross-price elasticities is so sparse that inter-commodity effects cannot be predicted with accuracy. (For instance, if full account could be taken of all livestock and grain production and consumption effects, net exports of barley might rise rather than fall.) Fourthly, the small country assumption sometimes made may not hold for all commodities. Fifth, it is rare that account is taken of the effect on trade of the *form* of the interventions by which domestic production is supported, albeit that different instruments of policy that provide the same degree of protection can have very different trade volume and price effects (deGorter and McClatchy, 1984) and different impacts on

TABLE CN-7

**Effect on Agricultural Trade Balance of
Abandoning Support to Agriculture, Canada, 1980**

| | | NET AGRICULTURAL TRADE BALANCE ($ Can. billions) | | | |
| | | EXCLUDING TERMS OF TRADE EFFECT | | INCLUDING TERMS OF TRADE EFFECT[5] | |
SCENARIO[1]	ADJUSTED[2] EFFECTIVE PROTECTION RATE (%)	LOW ELASTICITY[3]	HIGH ELASTICITY[4]	LOW ELASTICITY[3]	HIGH ELASTICITY[4]
A	15	1.5	0.6	2.0	1.8
B	30	0.9	−0.9	1.8	1.1
C	37	0.7	−1.0	1.6	1.0

The actual net agricultural trade balance in 1980 was 2.6.

[1]Scenarios A, B and C, as in Table CN-5.

[2]ERP shown for 1980 in Table CN-5 adjusted for the effects of quota restrictions on output or marketings in milk, eggs, poultry meats, tobacco, grains and oilseeds.

[3]Aggregate elasticity 0.2, demand elasticity −0.25.

[4]Aggregate supply elasticity 0.5, demand elasticity −0.25.

[5]International price elasticity of demand of −5.0 for net trade in agricultural production from Canada.

Source: Lattimore (1982), Tables 4.2 and 4.4.

international market stability (Bales and Lutz, 1979). Finally—and particularly relevant for this trilateral report—no account is taken in these estimates of changes in product (and input) prices of multilateral adjustments in national farm programs and associated frontier measures, though unilateral withdrawal of support for Canadian agriculture and liberalization of foreign access to the Canadian food market is implausible. The OECD study referred to above is considering the agricultural trade effects of a reduction in Canadian agricultural protection in a multi-commodity and multi-country framework. Not surprisingly, the preliminary results of the OECD research show effects on Canadian agricultural commodity production, consumption and trade that are different from—and smaller and more easily accommodated than—the magnitudes indicated by the partial and episodic national studies reported here.

REFERENCES

Agriculture Canada, *Orientation of Canadian Agriculture*, A Task Force Report (Ottawa: 1977).

Agriculture Canada, *Food and Agriculture Sector: Industry Analysis Report*, paper prepared for the National Economic Development Conference, Ottawa, January 1980.

Agriculture Canada, *Challenge for Growth: An Agri-food Strategy for Canada*, AGR-6-81DP (Ottawa: July 1981).

Agriculture Canada, *Review of the Western Grain Stabilization Act* (Ottawa: Program Evaluation Branch, February 1984).

Agriculture Canada, *Proposed Red Meat Stabilization Program* (Ottawa: March 4, 1984).

Agriculture Canada, *Canada's Trade in Agricultural Products 1981, 1982, and 1983* (Ottawa: Supply and Services Canada, October 1984).

Agriculture Canada, *Evaluation of the Market Risks Programs* (Ottawa: Program Evaluation Branch, October 1984).

M.D. Bales and E. Lutz, "The Effects of Trade Intervention on International Price Instability," *American Journal of Agricultural Economics* (61), 1979.

R.R. Barichello, "Government Policies in Support of Canadian Agriculture: Their Costs," unpublished paper prepared for a workshop of the U.S.-Canada International Agricultural Trade Research Consortium, Airlie House, Virginia, December 1982.

G.L. Brinkman and J.A. Gellner, "Relative Rates of Resource Returns for Ontario Commercial Farmers: A Farm to Non-farm Comparison, 1971-1974," *Canadian Journal of Agricultural Economics*, July 1977.

G.L. Brinkman, *Farm Incomes in Canada* (Ottawa: Supply and Services Canada, 1981).

J.D. Forbes, D.R. Hughes and T.K. Warley, *Economic Intervention and Regulation in Canadian Agriculture*, Supply and Services Canada for the Economic Council of Canada and the Institute for Research on Public Policy (Ottawa: 1982).

H. deGorter and D. McClatchy, "Reflections on the OECD Study Evaluating the Impacts of Agricultural Policies on Trade," unpublished paper presented to the U.S.-Canada International Agricultural Trade Research Consortium Workshop, Wye Woods, August 1984.

D.R. Harvey, *Christmas Turkey or Prairie Vulture? An Economic Analysis of the Crow's Nest Pass Grain Rates* (Montreal: Institute for Research on Public Policy, 1980).

R.G. Lattimore, "Canadian Agricultural Trade Policy: Commercial Market Relationships and Effect on the Level and Stability of World Prices," unpublished paper prepared for a workshop of the U.S.-Canada International Agricultural Trade Research Consortium, Airlie House, Virginia, December 1982.

Ontario Milk Marketing Board, "An Assessment of the Economic Council of Canada Report on Reforming Regulation with regard to Milk and Dairy Products" (Toronto: 1 July 1981, mimeo).

E.F. Whelan and A.C. Abbott, *A Food Strategy for Canada* (Ottawa:1977).

E.F. Whelan, *Issues for the Agri-sector to 2000*, submission to the Royal Commission on the Economic Union and Development Prospects for Canada (Regina: November 1983).

C. THE COMMON AGRICULTURAL POLICY OF THE EUROPEAN COMMUNITY[1]

The Beginning

The European Economic Community was established by the Treaty of Rome in March 1957. In Article 39 of the Treaty the objectives of the Common Agricultural Policy (CAP) are defined as follows:

- to increase agricultural productivity by promoting technical progress and by ensuring the rational development of agricultural production and the optimum utilization of the factors of production, in particular labor;
- thus to ensure a fair standard of living for the agricultural community, in particular by increasing the individual earnings of persons engaged in agriculture;
- to stabilize markets;
- to assure the availability of supplies;
- to ensure that supplies reach consumers at reasonable prices.

In addition, in the chapter on commercial policy, Article 110 stipulates that the establishment of a customs union between member states should contribute to the harmonious development of world trade, the progressive abolition of restrictions on international trade and the lowering of customs barriers.

In July 1958, at the so-called Stresa Conference, the signatories of the Treaty enlarged on the objectives defined in the Treaty and set guidelines for the CAP:

- The structures of European agriculture were to be reformed to become more competitive, without any threat to family farms.
- As production costs were higher in the Community than in the other main producing countries, the common prices were to provide adequate earnings and were to be established above world prices, without this being an incentive to overproduction.
- The Common Agricultural Policy could not be autarchic but was to protect the internal market against distortion by outside competition.

These were the foundations for the basic instruments of the CAP, namely regulation of markets and prices, regulation of external relations and reform of structures. It should be observed, however, that so long as the CAP has been in existence, the emphasis has been on market and price policy. Right from the start a main objective of the CAP has been to give the farmer an adequate income through the market, maintained by minimum prices.

Basic Principles of the CAP

The agricultural common market is based essentially on three principles on which the Common Agricultural Policy is founded: market unity, Community preference and joint financial responsibility.

Market Unity

Market unity between the member states allows products to circulate freely, without customs duty, equivalent charges or subsidies which distort competition; it requires the

---

[1]This text is partly based on information, documents and statistical material of the Community, the OECD secretariat, Eurostat and GATT. For the readableness of this essay the material is sometimes simplified and statistical problems are not mentioned.

common organization of markets and the introduction of common prices, the harmonization of administrative, health protection and veterinary regulations and stable currency parities within the EC. The principle of market unity underlies the concept that the elimination of internal protection and the introduction of common protective measures at the frontiers should result in a single price for every product within the Community. Regional price differences would, of course, exist but would generally correspond to the cost of transport between the regions and the consumer centers. The single price would be arrived at by competition between farms and regions and would lead to changes in the structure of the sector. Farms and regions should specialize on the basis of their comparative advantages, with the result that some farms and products would expand at the expense of others with higher production costs. However, as concern over farmers' earnings went hand in hand with the need to maintain a certain level of economic activity in the less favored regions, administrative action was taken to set prices high enough to maintain a certain level of income even for farms with high production costs. The consequence has been that the available factors of production have been allocated in such a way as to generate surpluses which have become too costly for the Community budget to dispose of on the world market. A great deal of work has been done, and is continuing, on harmonizing national regulations, but harmonization has not been achieved in many areas; there are numerous technical and legislative obstacles which all have the same effect as quantitative restrictions on trade.

Community Preference
Community preference means that Community farm produce has priority for sale on the internal market over imports from non-member countries. This is achieved partly by regulating machinery, which operates like a sluice-gate for imports and exports and absorbs price variations at the external boundaries of the Community. In addition, Community preference can be achieved directly by customs duties and also internally by production subsidies within the Community. This preference is limited, first by international obligations entered into by the Community, particularly within GATT, and secondly by preferential agreements concluded with non-member countries. Some of the products covered by these commitments are in fact being used increasingly as substitutes for European products and some member countries see this as a departure from the basic principle. This being so, the Council has recently taken a number of decisions concerning imports, which are designed to ensure "proper respect for Community preference".

Common Financial Responsibility
Common financial responsibility has two elements: first, the funds required for the Common Agricultural Policy are provided jointly and, secondly, the revenue produced by the operation of the policy (import levies or duties, production levies, etc.) constitute the Community's own resources. This principle is given practical expression in the European Agricultural Guidance and Guarantee Fund (EAGGF) which is an integral part of the Community budget. This fund has two sections: the "Guarantee" section used in particular to finance government expenditure arising from the common agricultural market organizations and the "Guidance" section which provides funds for the reform of agricultural structures.

Implementation of the CAP

Markets and Price Policy
Once the objectives and basic principles of the Common Agricultural Policy had been defined, the necessary market organizations were set up. Originally, these organizations

covered more than half the agricultural production of the Six. By 1970, the figure was 87 percent and now almost all the major products are covered by common market organizations; there are, however, two exceptions—the Commission's proposals for potatoes and alcohol have not yet been approved by the Council of Ministers.

The common market organizations, based on the common price system, involve the removal of barriers to intra-Community trade, the establishment of common frontier regulations for both imports and exports and the application of common rules for competition. These common market organizations fall into four main categories, using different mechanisms:

- Support prices cover over 72 percent of production (most cereals, sugar, milk, beef and veal, pig meat, certain fruits and vegetables, table wine and fishery products). The support price is the minimum price on the internal market. If the market price falls to the minimum price level, intervention mechanisms become operative; however, these take different forms in the individual market organizations.
- Straightforward protection against non-Community products covers 25 percent of production (flowers, other wine, other fruits and vegetables, eggs and poultry). This external protection may take the form of levies, which are calculated differently for each market organization, or customs duties, or a combination of the two. There are also various special measures to deal with particularly critical situations.
- Supplementary product aid, similar to the old British deficiency payments, covers only 2.5 percent of production (durum wheat, olive oil, some oilseeds, tobacco).
- Flat-rate aid based on acreage or output covers less than 1 percent of production (cotton seed, flax seed and hemp seed, hops, silkworms, seed and dehydrated fodder).

The different forms of market organization, geared to give the required output and guarantees have led to the emergence of a number of different price concepts. First, prices for the main purpose of managing the domestic market (target price, guide price, intervention price, etc.) give rise to internal measures (intervention, producer aids, etc.) and, secondly, prices which are directly related to the previous group and serve basically as an instrument of Community protection and preference in relation to outside markets (threshold price, sluice-gate price, etc.) give rise to frontier measures (levies, refunds, etc.). The various price supports, protection systems and producer aids have generally been applied to unlimited amounts of production and have contributed, in differing degree according to product, to a substantial increase in agricultural production, resulting in surpluses in some cases.

Measures affecting imports. In the case of most Community agricultural products there is no customs duty on imports from non-member countries and the common organization of markets and prices is based on the setting of a target price, an intervention price and a threshold price. In order to guarantee Community producers a level of prices generally above world market prices and to protect internal markets against the erratic variations of world prices, a variable levy is charged on imports from outside the Community. These levies (which match the difference between c.i.f. import prices and the threshold prices) bring world supply prices up to the target prices, taking account of internal transport costs. The products to which this system applies in full are cereals, rice, olive oil, sugar, milk and milk products.

Measures influencing exports. Refunds are the basic instruments for exports. They are to some extent the counterpart of levies and are used to ensure Community products a competitive position for outlets in non-member countries. European producers are refunded the difference between the internal market price (including costs of transport to the Community port of export) and the selling price obtainable on the world market. However, in addition to this price difference, the amount of the refund also depends on the destination and on the situation at the time. Refunds are the same for all the Community and are met out of the Community's agricultural budget except in the case of sugar for which, since 1 July 1981, they have been wholly paid by producers in the form of a production levy.

A "classical" example. One of the first market organizations to be introduced was that for cereals, in 1962. It was regarded from the beginning as, in effect, a "model." It has since been revised in many respects, but for our present purpose we can confine ourselves to a simplified basic model to explain the principal mechanisms. The situation for wheat has been chosen for illustration.

The target price is the linchpin of the market organization. It is set at the beginning of each year as being the producer price desirable in terms of agricultural policy. If the domestic supply exceeds demand, the market price—i.e., the actual producer price—usually falls below the target price. If the fall in price reaches a certain critical point, the Community intervenes to stabilize the market, purchasing the producers' wheat at a pre-determined price. This is called the intervention price, because public authority "intervenes" on the market at this price through intervention agencies set up specifically for the purpose. The intervention price is well below the target price. It forms the lower limit for domestic prices and represents a kind of guaranteed minimum price for Community producers. It is a cornerstone of the system.

The intra-Community prices for wheat are usually higher than the prices of the other major world producers of wheat (United States, Canada and Australia), whose production conditions are much more favorable. To prevent the Community market from being

FIGURE EC-1

Levy and Refund System for Wheat

flooded from outside in this situation, which would result in the complete collapse of European production, and to enable Community producers to participate in world trade, regulatory measures have to be taken at the boundaries of the Community. For this reason, a threshold price is set for imports and the lower import price (world market price plus transport to Community frontier) is increased to that level. The threshold price is calculated so that the price of the imported wheat at the major consumption centers of the Community, including transport and unloading costs, roughly corresponds to the target price. The difference between the threshold price and the import price is charged as a "levy" and accrues to the Community budget as a contribution to the Community's own financial resources. Conversely, when European producers export, they are refunded the difference between the market price in the Community (including transport costs to port of export in the Community) and the possible selling price on the world market. The refunds are met from the agricultural budget of the Community.

Structural Policy
Structural diversity in every respect has from the beginning been one of the main features of European agriculture: differences in natural production conditions (soil and climate); differences in farm sizes, specialization and production methods; differences in age and educational level of the farmers; and differences in development outside agriculture—in the economic and social context. All these differences had arisen and become intensified and consolidated over the centuries in the isolation of Europe's individual nation-states. They still persist today to a substantial extent and have been exacerbated by the enlargements of the Community in 1973 and 1981.

Until the beginning of the 1970s, virtually every member country tried to tackle its problems of agricultural structure individually. At the Community level, efforts were concentrated on merely coordinating the various national policies. In addition, some individual projects were financed from a common fund (the "Guidance" section of the EAGGF). An initial outline for a truly common structural policy was only drawn up towards the end of the 1960s. Since then the structural policy of the Community has centered on three main fields: the farmer and his farm, the marketing and processing of agricultural products, and the reduction of regional discrepancies. The policies have concentrated on: utilization of technical progress, modernization of farms and rationalization of production. Programs were developed for interest rate reductions or capital grants for modernization of farms, special help for young starting farmers and the retirement of older farmers.

For a long time the Community had confined itself to the isolated funding of individual projects, but in the second half of the 1970s, it began increasingly to concentrate on the promotion of comprehensive and coherent sectoral or regional development programs in the member states. Community grants can be made available in respect of measures for the marketing of agricultural products (e.g., packaging plants for fruits and vegetables) and the processing of products (e.g., slaughterhouses and wineries) covered by such programs. Some changes of emphasis are called for in the structural policy. The available resources should be applied preferentially to the weaker farms and in the disadvantaged regions.

Regional Policy
The desire of the Community to foster a greater degree of economic convergence throughout the EC has led to a number of initiatives in the field of regional policy. The broad aim of regional policy in the EC is to promote harmonized development within the Community by action designed to raise levels of economic performance in the poorer regions and hence to reduce the differentials which exist between regions (Treaty of

Rome, Preamble). Most significantly, the European Regional Development Fund (ERDF) was established in 1975. However, the resources allocated to regional policy currently account for only about 10 percent of the total Community budget; the major source of regional expenditure is national budgets, being about 95 percent of the total.

At the Community level there are three broad strands of regional policy:

- First there are the "regional dimensions" in other EC policies. These include agriculture, industry, trade and social policies. The objective is to take account of the regional dimension in these policies. In 1979, the Commission made proposals on policy with regard to agricultural structures, particularly those relating to Integrated Development Programmes which were viewed as a way of providing aid for agricultural areas which at the same time could contribute to a reduction in regional differentials in standards of living throughout the Community.
- The second strand of policy involves those at the national level. The Community's objective is to coordinate such policies by fixing ceilings for national aids for investment in development areas and to harmonize those regional programs that can benefit from EC funds for regional development.
- A third strand of policy specifically offers support through the ERDF to development areas.

Monetary Policy

Following the completion of the customs union and Common Agricultural Policy, towards the end of the 1960s, the objective of economic and monetary union appeared to be the next step in the Community's development. This was given extra emphasis with the subsequent breakdown of fixed exchange rates in the Bretton Woods system and the upheavals caused by the first oil price increase. These developments are of particular relevance to agriculture as the CAP was based on the assumption of fixed exchange rates. In the early years of the EC, prices determined in units of account by the EC for purposes of CAP intervention and trade were translated into national currencies at the prevailing fixed parities. However, when exchange rates changed in the late 1960s, the translation of CAP prices (until 1978 measured in units of account, thereafter in ECUs) into national currencies implied changes in support prices amongst the member states. Thus, in a country with a depreciating currency, support prices in national currency would have risen, and vice versa. As member countries considered it undesirable to allow domestic agricultural prices to change in this way, rates of exchange for agricultural purposes (representative or "green" rates) were established. In order to maintain the difference between the "market" and "green" rates, border taxes and subsidies (monetary compensatory amounts, MCAs) were used. Therefore, in a country with a depreciating currency, the "green" rate remained over-valued, domestic agricultural prices did not rise and a tax on agricultural exports (and subsidy on agricultural imports)—a so-called "negative MCA" —prevented intra-Community trade and currency arbitrage from circumventing and thus neutralizing the system.

In relation to extra-EC trade, export and import prices are similarly adjusted by the MCAs. Refunds on extra-EC exports from a country with a depreciating currency are reduced (taxed) and import levies are reduced (subsidized) by the amount of the MCA. The converse is the case for countries with appreciating currencies. During the 1970s, the range of MCAs between member countries was very high at times. However, the influence of the discipline provided by the European Monetary System (EMS)—established in March 1979—as well as possibly more settled international monetary conditions have, into the 1980s, considerably reduced this range. The longer-term objective of the Community is to completely eliminate "green" rates and MCAs in the agricultural sector.

Agricultural Evolution in the Community

Integration
The agricultural sector has become more and more integrated in the rest of the economy. For that reason general economic policies have become increasingly decisive for the income and adjustment possibilities of modern farming. For a better understanding of this influence three elements should be noted:
- Agriculture is not the only source of income for those working in agriculture. In European farming, only 30 percent of the farming population is fully employed in agriculture and 30 percent is employed for less than a quarter of a normal day's work. The access to and the situation of the "labor market" outside agriculture is of major importance to income and adjustment possibilities of the farming population.
- The modern farm has gradually integrated into large segments of the economy and buys 50 percent of the value of its production from "outside": energy, fertilizer, feed, capital costs, wages, etc. Because of this growing share of "intermediate consumption" farming has become more vulnerable to inflationary effects on the prices of these "intermediate" products. The negative influence (of inflation, rising energy costs, high interest rates, volatile exchange rates and rising unemployment) on real farm incomes has been felt in Europe since 1975. Agricultural price policies that try to compensate for these general trends may destabilize markets and cause substantial budgetary costs.
- Eighty percent of farm products have to be processed to be marketable to the consumer. Income and adjustment possibilities of the farmer are therefore geared to the market orientation of the food industry, its development and its degree of protection from international competition.

Agriculture's share in the Community's GDP is relatively small and falling continually. In 1982, it was about 3.6 percent as compared with around 5 percent in 1973 and 7 percent in 1960. This percentage should, however, be set against the figures for other sectors of the economy; the value of Community agriculture is of the same order as that of the chemicals industry plus plastics, which are looked upon as leading sectors of the Community's economy.

As stated earlier agriculture is progressively becoming more integrated, both upstream towards the factors of production and downstream towards the agri-foodstuff industries. Today agriculture and the food industry are so interwoven that they form an important economic complex with its own buoyancy for growth. This complex at present accounts for about 7.5 percent of Community GDP and provides more than 10 million jobs. There has been similar, increasing interpenetration between the agricultural sector and upstream sectors of the economy. This process, which makes a permanent contribution to the economic growth of the Community, has basically taken the form of faster gross fixed capital formation than in the economy as a whole and increased inputs. The value of inputs as a share of the value of final agricultural production has risen continuously and, as noted earlier, now stands at about 50 percent. Over the last ten years, the value of final agricultural production, at constant prices, has risen at an annual rate of slightly over 9 percent , as compared with about 11 percent for inputs. The biggest input item is "animal feedingstuffs" (44 percent in 1981) and this is followed by "fertilizers" (14 percent) and "energy" (11 percent).

The utilized agricultural area (EC-9) has fallen continuously by about 400,000 hectares annually, from 101.3 million hectares in 1960 to 92 million hectares in 1983. The drop in the labor force has been much greater; in 1960, 19.1 million people were employed in agriculture in the ten member countries of the Community, a figure which fell by an average of 4.5% annually up to 1970, when it stood at about 12 million; since then, even though the flight from the country has slowed down somewhat (an annual average of 2.5 percent), the agricultural labor force fell again by over 4 million to 8.0 million in 1983. This is still 7.7 percent of the whole working population. In addition, the amount of part-time work in agriculture is rising. It would be a mistake to think that all the drop in the utilized agricultural area and the loss of farm workers is solely attributable to a transfer of factors to other sectors of the economy, as land may be abandoned and deaths or retirements may reduce the labor force. Nevertheless, although varying by time and country, a relatively large fraction has been transferred to other sectors of the economy which in turn supply more to agriculture (machinery, fertilizers, pesticides, etc.).

The increase in agricultural gross value added, combined with the drop in farm employment, has led to an increase in productivity, putting agriculture among the leading sectors in the Community economy. From 1968 to 1975, labor productivity in the Community (of Nine) rose by an annual average of about 3.1 percent while the annual increase for agriculture was 6.3 percent, although with marked differences between regions. Also in the period 1975 to 1980, the figure for agriculture was more than double (4.8 percent).

Key Figures
The tremendous development of the agricultural sector in the EC is indicated by some key figures in Table EC-1 (these figures may only be seen as indications for the mentioned years).

TABLE EC-1

Key Figures for European Community Agriculture, 1962, 1973 and 1983

(EC-9)

	1962	1973	1983
Agriculture's share in GDP (%)	7	5	3.6
Agricultural area (million ha.)	101	93	92
Persons employed (x 1000)	17,000	10,500	7,000
Number of farms (x 1000)	8,500	5,200	4,600
Average hectares per farm	11	15	18
Average production per milk cow (kg/head)	2,950	3,550	4,430
Average production of wheat (100 kg/ha.)	25	35	52
Intra-EC agricultural trade ($ U.S. billion)	5	13	46[a]
Extra-EC agricultural exports ($ U.S. billion)	3	9	24[a]
Extra-EC agricultural imports ($ U.S. billion)	11	30	45[a]

[a]EC-10

Prices and Incomes
Community farmers have in general enjoyed the benefits of continuously rising farm producer prices. The increase differs, however, from country to country and year to year.

If the rise of agricultural prices over the period 1975-82 is compared with the rise of inflation in each member state (on the basis of the GDP deflator), it can be seen that farm producer prices fell in real terms in all member countries except Greece. The biggest drops were in the United Kingdom, the Netherlands and Italy; the smallest were in Denmark and Luxembourg.

In 1983, the cost of inputs as a percentage of the value of final agricultural production ranged from 24 percent in Greece to 58 percent in Belgium. The trend of input costs is a critical determinant of the trend of incomes. The increase in input prices followed much the same pattern as that of farm producer prices described above. Since 1975, the average increase in input prices has been a little below the rate of inflation in nearly every country.

On average, real farm incomes (measured by net agricultural value added per head of the labor force, in real terms) improved in all member states until 1973, but after the 1974 drop in earnings, movements differed from country to country. The rising trend was resumed in France, Italy and Ireland up to 1979; in Denmark the rise was again inter-

TABLE EC-2

EC Imports and Exports of Agricultural Products, by Trading Partner (EC-10)

	IMPORTS				EXPORTS			
	MILLION ECU		% OF TOTAL		MILLION ECU		% OF TOTAL	
	1973	1983	1973	1983	1973[a]	1983	1973[a]	1983
Total	40,361	102,579	—	—	22,639	78,775	—	—
Intra-EC	15,841	51,891	—	—	15,258	51,605	—	—
Extra-EC	24,520	50,362	100	100	7,381	26,766	100	100
United States	4,236	9,486	17.3	18.8	1,222	3,818	16.6	14.3
Japan	169	229	0.7	0.5	288	906	3.9	3.4
Western Europe (excluding EC)	2,519	5,344	10.3	10.6	1,725	4,482	23.4	16.7
Industrialized Commonwealth	3,467	4,614	14.1	9.2	341	1,116	4.6	4.2
Yugoslavia	359	621	1.5	1.2	118	251	1.6	0.9
State-trading countries	2,519	3,618	10.3	7.2	747	3,241	10.1	12.1
Mediterranean area	2,846	5,230	11.6	10.4	1,070	4,168	14.5	15.6
Spain	987	2,319	4.0	4.5	199	784	2.7	2.9
Portugal	184	404	0.7	0.8	63	132	0.9	0.5
Latin America, Central and South	3,867	9,089	15.7	18.0	259	656	3.5	2.5
ACP (Lomé Convention)	2,680	6,509	10.9	12.9	573	2,333	7.8	8.7
Other	1,858	5,622	7.6	11.2	1,038	5,795	14.0	21.6

[a]EC-9

rupted in 1978 and resumed subsequently; in the other countries, incomes fell in 1976 or 1977, and did not improve until 1981 in the case of Belgium and the Netherlands. In Greece, earnings rose regularly. In 1982, real incomes rose in all member states, with particularly sharp increases in Luxembourg (39 percent up on 1981), Denmark and France (19 percent up), Germany (16 percent up) and the United Kingdom (12 percent up).

Trade
With 1983 exports of 24 billion dollars and imports of 45 billion dollars, the Community's total external trade in agricultural products is larger than any of its trading partners. Since the first Community enlargement in 1973, an increasing share of agricultural exports has been accounted for by deliveries to ACP (Lomé Convention), state-trading and OPEC countries, compared to a decreasing share with other OECD countries (Table EC-2). With regard to the Community's agricultural imports, the United States, ACP countries, Latin America and non-OECD Asian countries have increased their shares relative to other OECD and state-trading countries. Although the enlargement of the Community in 1973 was a factor in the decrease in the relative importance of trade with Canada, Australia and New Zealand, it should be noted that this trend was already evident in the United Kingdom's trade pattern before accession.

Since 1970, final agricultural production in the Community has increased at around 2 percent annually, a rate about double that of consumption. This has had an even greater proportional effect on trends in extra-Community exports and imports. Since 1973 the proportion of EC production exported has increased and the proportion of consumption imported has decreased, significantly for several commodities. The notable exceptions to these trends are soybeans and rapeseed. Closely related to these developments, the Community has increased its share of world agricultural exports and decreased its respective share of imports. Between 1973 and 1982/83 the Community's share of world agricultural exports went from 10 percent to 11 percent, whilst EC imports decreased from 31 percent to 20 percent of total world exports (Table EC-3). The Community remains an important market for oils, fats, proteins, sheep meat and tropical fruits. It is a major world market supplier of dairy products, beef, sugar, wine, wheat flour and poultry meat.

Between 1973/74 and 1982/83 the self-sufficiency ratios for the main agricultural commodities increased considerably (Table EC-4).

TABLE EC-3

World Exports and EC External Trade
(EC-10, billion U.S. $)

	1973	1980	1983
World exports			
All products	465.5	1,631.8	1,507.1
of which: agricultural products	98.6	245.8	222.6
EC external trade			
Exports			
All products	100.1	310.5	269.8
of which: agricultural products	9.7	28.1	23.8
Imports			
All products	105.5	382.1	292.4
of which: agricultural products	30.5	59.8	44.8

TABLE EC-4

Degree of Self-Sufficiency of European Community
(percent)

	1962 (EC-6)	1973 (EC-9)	1983 (EC-9)
Wheat	100	104	125
Maize	n.a.	56	72
Sugar	97	91	144
Cheese	98	102	108
Butter	101	101	123
Beef and veal	87	91	104
Pigmeat	99	101	101
Poultry	98	103	110
Fruit	86	79	81
Vegetables	112	94	97

The observed trends in output and trade occurred during a period—as in all OECD countries—of slow economic growth, high rates of inflation and global structural change. Whilst Community policies may have lessened the impact of these developments in the agricultural sector, structural changes that were apparent long before the economic crises during the 1970s continued to have an effect. Between 1970 and 1983 the number of people employed in the agricultural sector, as noted above, fell by 4 million, a 33 percent decrease. The average size of farms continued to grow, as did the importance of purchased inputs, and by the beginning of the 1980s one-quarter of all farms were producing three-quarters of total agricultural output.

Budgetary Consequences
The budget of the EC is only about 26 billion ECU, which is the same as that of one of the states in Western Germany. The expenditures for agricultural policy account for about 70 percent of this budget. The expenditures of the Guarantee section of the European Agricultural Guidance and Guarantee Fund (EAGGF) are generally classified as the costs of the price and market policy of the EC. The share of EAGGF expenditures in the whole budget has declined a few percentage points in the last 10 years to less than 68 percent in 1984.

When expenditure is broken down by commodity sector, the high proportion accounted for by a few products is obvious (Table EC-5). This reflects the problem with structural surpluses in the supply of certain agricultural products.

Regarding the costs of the price and market policy of the EC besides the expenditures of the EAGGF, (indirect) support from national governments for agriculture can also come under this heading. It appears that the total expenditure on agriculture in the EC in the period 1979 to 1983 came to about 1.5 percent of the GNP.

Changes in the CAP
The upheavals of the years 1980-84 forced the Community to reconsider some basic elements of the CAP and embark on a gradual program of reform and tackle its major problem areas, notably in the dairy and the cereals sectors. The wine and olive oil sectors have become an increasing problem in view of existing surpluses and the Community's

TABLE EC-5

EAGGF Expenditures, Guarantee Section
(million ECU)

	1973/1975[a]		1984	
		%		%
Dairy	1,345	35.0	5,811	31.6
Cereals	675	17.5	1,935	10.5
Beef and veal	421	11.0	2,056	11.2
Sugar	173	4.5	1,602	8.7
Fruit and vegetables	52	1.5	1,343	7.3
Wine	64	1.5	1,082	6.0
Olive oil	172	4.5	888	4.8
Oils and fats	41	1.0	864	4.1
Other	690	18.0	2,410	13.6
	3,633	94.5	17,991	97.8
MCAs	212	5.5	410	2.2
	3,845	100.0	18,401	100.0

[a]Annual average over three years.

enlargement to include Spain and Portugal. In the following paragraphs, attention will be focused on the major elements of the Community's intended policies of adjustment and their implications for two major commodities: milk and cereals.

The stagnation and decline in demand, both in the Community and in external markets, led the Community to the following line for future policies: "It is no longer reasonable to provide unlimited guarantees of price and intervention when there is doubt about the possibility of outlets in the coming years. In other words, Europe's agricultural producers must understand that they will have to participate more fully in the cost of disposing of products beyond a certain threshold. The measures necessary to ensure respect for such guarantee thresholds constitute the centrepiece (of the reform of the CAP)....Alongside the introduction of guarantee thresholds, the (European) Commission considers it necessary to pursue a restrictive price policy".[2] With this policy shift, the Community has made a major attempt to reduce its structural surpluses to manageable proportions and to alleviate pressure on the world market for which it has a major responsibility.

Milk
In a major shift in Community policy, it was decided in 1984 to limit guarantees of milk deliveries to about 99.2 million tons for the year 1984-85 and to 98.1 million tons annually for the period 1985-89. Deliveries above this threshold will be "penalized" by a levy of 75 percent (per farm) or 100 percent (per factory) of the milk target price. This decision means that Community milk deliveries have to be reduced by 5 percent compared to deliveries of 103.5 million tons in 1983. Alongside these measures, the general milk tax (co-responsibility levy) on farmers to finance surpluses was increased from 2 percent to 3 percent together with a price freeze. The result of this drastic change in policy will be a decline in real incomes in the dairy sector of about 10 percent in 1984 and 1985.

---

[2]Commission of the European Communities, "Common Agricultural Policy, Proposals of the Commission," COM (83) 500 (Brussels: 28 July 1983, mimeo), pp. 8,9.

For the purposes of this report it is not feasible to go into the details of this new policy; however, it should be noted that this policy has consequences for:

- employment in the dairy sector and related industries;
- sales of animal feed;
- the balance of the beef market because of accelerated marketing of redundant cows (temporary effect);
- the structure of dairy production at the farm level;
- land prices.

Cereals

Also in the case of wheat there has been a major shift in the policy. The following policy is being pursued:

- A limitation of guarantees to a threshold of 121.32 million tons of cereals for the year 1984-85. The threshold will be increased to the extent that imports of cereal substitutes exceed 15 million tons. For each 1 million tons of cereals (excluding durum) by which the threshold is exceeded, the prices will be lowered by 1 percent, up to a maximum of 5 percent. With an expected harvest of approximately 145 million tons in 1984-85, this means that the Community prices for cereals will be automatically reduced by 5 percent in 1985-86. For 1984-85 the prices were lowered by 1 percent. This policy was started in 1982.
- A price policy to strengthen the competitive position of EC cereals on the world market and to promote internal consumption. The aim is to align Community prices with those of its major competitors.
- Stabilizing of duty-free imports of cereal substitutes through voluntary agreements.

Conclusion

The Community's agricultural sector has been very successful in raising the level of production for most of its commodities. The CAP has ensured an environment in which policy has underpinned producer prices that have for most products increased steadily, have been consistently above world levels and have offered a climate conducive to investment. The Community objectives of security of supplies and stability of markets have been amply achieved. However, as the increase in Community consumption has failed to match the pace set by production increases (few of the demand stimulants of low prices, growing populations, rising incomes and diets in need of improvement were evident during the last decade), the corollary has been growing supplies of commodities searching for external markets and a shrinkage of the Community's own market for imports. The budgetary costs have been substantial and as the surpluses of cereals, dairy products, beef, olive oil and wine have increased, so have the associated costs of their disposal. In 1982 and 1983, Community expenditure on market support rose considerably. Whilst expenditure on export refunds has eased with the rise in the exchange rate of the U.S. dollar *vis-à-vis* the ECU, it has risen with the growth of intervention stocks.

The Community has now embarked on the road which should lead, in the medium term, to a lowering of real prices and a further participation in the costs of exports by farmers as a means for translating developments on the world market into the decisions of farmers.

D. AGRICULTURAL POLICY IN JAPAN

Present agricultural policy consists of two groups of programs; one originating in agrarian Japan and the other in developed Japan. The Staple Food Control Program of 1942, the Land Reform Program of 1946 and the Agricultural Cooperative Programs of 1948 belong to the former group. When these were launched primary industry formed about a quarter of Japan's gross national product and employed about half of her total labor force. Food was in severe short supply, and consumers were spending more than half of their total consumption expenditure on food. After 1955 both the agricultural and non-agricultural economies were reconstructed from the war damage, and food shortages had disappeared. Adjustment to the growing Japanese economy became the central agricultural problem. (Recent development of Japanese agriculture is indicated by some key figures in Table JN-1.) The Basic Agricultural Act of 1961 was designed to increase productivity of labor in agriculture by improving the basic structure of the agricultural

TABLE JN-1

Key Figures for Japanese Agriculture, 1970, 1980 and 1983

	1970	1980	1983
Agriculture's share in GDP (%)[a]	6.1	3.8	3.3
Agricultural area (million ha.)	5.8	5.5	5.4
Persons employed (x 1000)	10,352	6,973	6,462
Employed mainly in farming (x 1000)	(7,109)	(4,128)	(4,031)
Number of farms (x 1000)	5,402	4,661	4,522
Excluding part-time farms (x 1000)	(2,659)	(1,652)	(1,327)
Average hectares per farm	1.07	1.17	1.20
Gross income per household ($ U.S.)[b]	4,365	24,147	26,891
from farm income (%)	(31.9)	(17.0)	(15.3)
from non-farm income (%)	(55.6)	(63.7)	(63.8)
seasonal migrators, pensions, etc. (%)	(12.5)	(19.3)	(20.9)
Average production per milk cow (kg/head)[c]	3,974	4,574	4,794
Average production of rice (brown) (100 kg/ha.)	43.4	44.6[d]	45.6
Average production of wheat (100 kg/ha.)	20.7	30.5	30.4
Exports of foodstuffs ($ U.S. billion)	0.6	1.6	1.4
Imports of foodstuffs ($ U.S. billion)	2.6	14.7	14.9

[a]Includes forestry and fisheries.
[b]Calculated by K. Hemmi.
[c]Two years or older.
[d]1979-81 average, since 1980 crop was extraordinarily bad.

Sources: Research Bureau, Economic Planning Agency, *Statistical Handbook, 1985* (in Japanese); Statistics and Information Bureau, Ministry of Agriculture, Forestry and Fisheries, *Statistical Handbook, 1984* (in Japanese).

sector, to adjust agricultural production to the changing demand situation, and to reduce the number of farms. The goal was one million "viable" farms by 1970, whose average productivity would yield the farmer the equivalent of an urban worker in income. This meant that at least 1.2 million farmers, out of a total of 6 million, would have to leave farming in ten years. Programs under the Basic Agricultural Act form the second group.

Although the programs of the 1940s, especially the Staple Food Control Program, have adjusted to the growing Japanese economy since 1955, the basic structure of these programs has been maintained to today. These aim at encouraging as many mini-size owner-operators as possible to remain in farming and at producing as much output as technologically possible. The primary objective of the latter group of programs is to assure fair income to the farmers, either by increasing farm productivity or by supporting agricultural prices. When foods are in abundant supply both domestically and internationally, increasing productivity is stressed. When food is in tight supply, price support is stressed. Japanese agricultural policy has swung between the poles of increasing food supplies (or food security) and increasing productivity (or production in line with comparative advantage). From 1960 to 1973, policy emphasized increasing productivity. After the "grain crisis"—especially the soybean embargo by the United States—and the establishment of a 200-mile fishing zone in many of the world's waters, the emphasis shifted towards increasing food supply. Since 1980 the policy has gradually swung toward increasing productivity again.

Food Security
For various reasons the stability, adequacy, and security of the supply of basic foods to consumers *at reasonable prices* has received special attention in all countries. Food prices are a major mover of the consumer price index, especially in low income countries. What requires special treatment here are the following two facts. First, in every country consumers take much more notice of food price movements than food price levels relative to other countries. They experience changes in food prices in their everyday life, whereas they have only poor knowledge of food prices in other countries. Food supply at reasonable prices usually means food supply *at stable prices*, and not at reasonably low levels. Second, food supply and prices in the world market are beyond the control of individual governments, especially of the countries having poor agricultural resources. These governments easily assume that a reliable supply of domestically produced foods and feeds is the most important one among various objectives of agricultural policy in their countries. In particular, countries with relatively low levels of self-sufficiency in food and feed production normally want to maintain certain levels of farm production, some of them even at a very high cost. Since Japan is the only country having a declining and very low level of food self-sufficiency (see Figure JN-1) among the trilateral countries, Japan stands out in asserting the food security issue in our three regions. Moreover, Japanese are very pessimistic about the future supply of food in the world. Without change in this opinion of the general public, the Japanese government has to continue to stress the food security issue.

Although Japanese consumers are most generous with regard to the high costs of agricultural support programs, especially of the rice support program, we have to take note of the exceedingly high costs of the present food security policy. In order to reduce the costs of agricultural support programs, the Japanese government has pursued the program of increasing productivity and efficiency of farm production and marketing. The government declared the policy goal of achieving producer prices comparable to Western European levels in some key commodities. The government has tried to reconcile two objectives: the food security objective and the objective to meet the requests of food exporting countries to open the Japanese market. We believe that the Japanese government has to pursue the above policy efforts much further. Although we are sympathetic to the Japanese concern with food security, we are very serious about the costs of programs for attaining food security. For example, if the average rice field could be increased from the present 0.6 hectare to 10.0 hectares per grower, the cost of producing one ton of rice would be less than a half (possibly a third) of the present one. Even without a ton of imports of rice, the rice price in Japan would be far lower than the present one if the government did not intervene in the domestic market.

In order to reduce the costs of attaining and maintaining food security, Japanese consumers and taxpayers should be better informed of the costs of maintaining present ways of attaining food security and of long-term trends in demand for and supply of foods in the OECD countries. A non-rice grain stockpiling program, to take another example, would be much more cost effective than the present wheat-barley program. The new program might be a combination of an enlarged government security stock and private stockpiling with a moderate government subsidy. Stockpiling policies for processed foods—canned, dried and frozen—can be adopted for attaining security of supply of perishable food products. We believe that the food security programs above, which are more market-oriented than present ones, would be more cost effective than the present programs.

Other trilateral countries can contribute to Japanese food security efforts. If these countries change their agricultural policies into more market-oriented ones as recommended in the final chapter of the foregoing report, the world markets for basic foods will be more stable. By assuring reasonable fishing rights to Japan in their 200-mile fishing zones, other countries can mitigate Japanese fear of food shortages since half of the supply of animal protein in Japan is provided by fish.

FIGURE JN-1

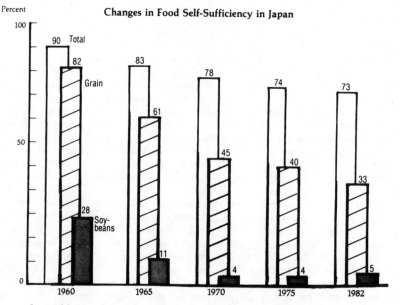

Percent

Changes in Food Self-Sufficiency in Japan

Source: Ministry of Agriculture, Forestry and Fisheries, *Food Balance Sheet*.

Swings in Agricultural Policy

The swings in agricultural policy referred to earlier can be seen through a comparative study of government forecasts of future demand and supply of various food commodities. There are four forecasts: 1959-71, 1966-77, 1972-85 and 1983-90. The last one was published in November 1980. Of course, it is not yet possible to examine the last forecast's accuracy, although actual acreage and production and consumption of the commodities concerned in the last five years have seemed to be in line with the fourth forecast. Major features of the first three forecasts are compared with realized figures in Figures JN-2 through JN-5. It should be noted that none of these forecasts represents a projection or target of government production programs. Instead, they show future demand and supply levels of food commodities desired by the government, and at the same time are based on past trends.

Figure JN-2 shows that the government overestimated future rice consumption in each of the first three forecasts. We must be sympathetic to the government's overestimating future consumption in the first forecast since there was no declining trend in per capita rice consumption before 1960. It seems that the government learned a lesson from the first several years of the first forecast period and, in the second forecast, adjusted the future per capita consumption trend to the actual trend. However, after the "grain crisis," the government overestimated future per capita rice consumption again; i.e., the government was more conservative in the third forecast than in the second forecast.

Figure JN-3 shows that the government underestimated future per capita wheat consumption in the first and third forecasts but was more realistic in the second forecast. Figure JN-3 shows the results of the government wheat production expansion program adopted after the "grain crisis."

FIGURE JN-2

Rice Consumption and Production, Forecasted and Actual

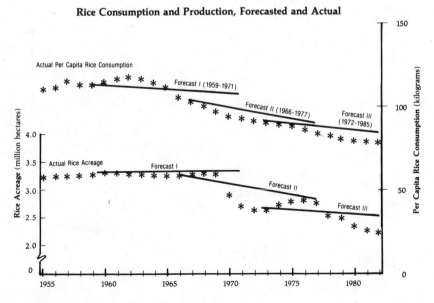

Figure JN-5 shows that both consumption and production trends for milk and milk products have slowed down successively, and also that the government forecasts have adjusted to these changes in the actual trends. Figure JN-4 is the most interesting. It shows that the government underestimated future meat consumption and production levels radically in the third forecast, after being more realistic in the first and the second forecasts. The author cannot understand why the Japanese government became very conservative in the third forecast in forecasting future consumption of rice, wheat and meats.

The government's "Basic Guidelines of Government Agricultural Policy in 1980," published in November 1980, will guide Japanese agriculture policy for several more years. There are two themes to the guidelines: the discussion of Japanese food consumption patterns and the adoption of the target of raising Japanese agricultural productivity to the level of the countries of the European Community. The discussion of Japanese food consumption patterns makes two assumptions. First, it is desirable to maintain the

FIGURE JN-3

Wheat Consumption and Production, Forecasted and Actual

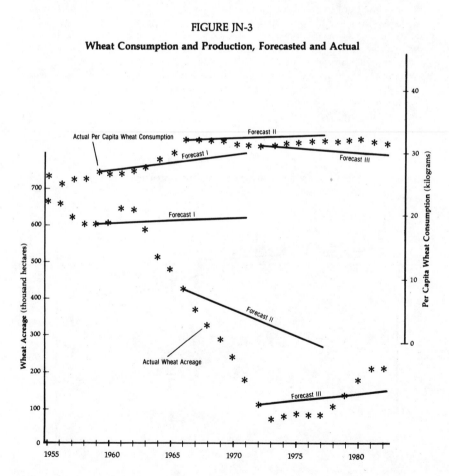

present level of per capita calorie intake—2,500 calories a day—and to maintain the current ratio of intake of the major nutrients—proteins 12-13 percent, fats 20-30 percent and carbohydrates 68-57 percent. The present level and pattern of Japanese food consumption is said to be ideal for human health. The second assumption is that it is desirable to consume locally produced foods. To maintain the present level and pattern of Japanese food consumption is desirable not only for health reasons but also for food security. It is sure that the conservative attitude of the government shown in Forecast III, especially with regard to meat consumption, culminated in this view of Japan's food consumption pattern. This view explains why the government is so strict in demanding complete self-sufficiency in rice, and why the government is so adamant in asserting that future Japanese meat consumption will not be much above the present level. The government projects that per capita annual meat consumption will be 26-28 kilograms in 1990 and 32-35 kilograms in 2000, compared to 24 kilograms currently.

Another aspect of Japanese agricultural policy is the very high level of price supports, shown in Table 1 in the foregoing report. In all cases the nominal rate of protection is higher than the producer support ratio since the denominator in the former (the border price) is smaller than the denominator in the latter (the domestic price) while the numerator is the same in both cases. Three trends are apparent. First, the support levels have increased steadily during the past 25 years. Japanese support levels were lower than those of EC countries in 1955. Japanese support levels were almost the same as those of EC countries in 1960. However, they were much higher than those of EC countries in

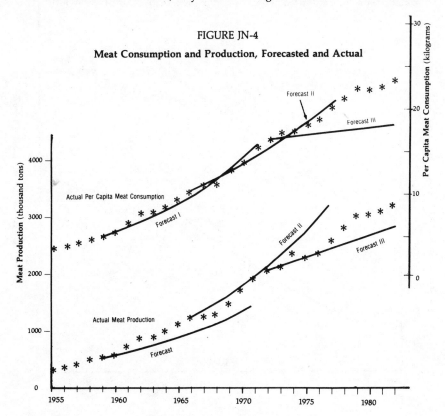

FIGURE JN-4

Meat Consumption and Production, Forecasted and Actual

1970. The increase in support levels was caused by both increases in domestic prices of the commodities concerned and by changes in the exchange rate of the yen *vis-à-vis* European currencies. Second, support levels for grains have always been much higher than those for livestock products. There appear to be two reasons for this difference. The main reason is that Japanese farmers have generally fed animals and chickens with imported feeds. Therefore, the levels in Table 1 do not show the effective rate of protection for livestock at all. The second reason is that government rice price supports—the most important of the grains—have never been severely criticized, either by rice exporting countries or by Japanese consumers. In a number of rice exporting countries, domestic rice prices are held below international market levels. If there were liberalization, bringing higher domestic prices, rice consumption would fall and rice production would increase in these countries. Therefore, many argue the *status quo* in the world rice market is good for these countries (see Appendix, Section E). The third point to be drawn from Table 1 is that support levels for livestock products did increase from 1970 to 1975 while support levels for grains did not increase in the same period. During this period prices of livestock products were marked up along with the increases in prices of imported feeds.

As stated earlier, the second theme of the "Basic Guidelines of Government Agricultural Policy" is the adoption of the target of increasing Japanese agricultural productivity to the

FIGURE JN-5

Consumption and Production of Milk and Milk Products, Forecasted and Actual

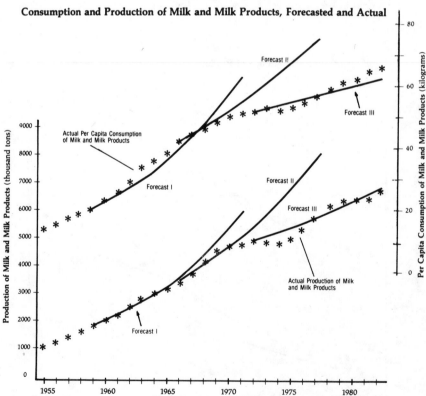

level of EC countries. As also stated earlier, at the beginning of the 1960s it was desired that, at the end of the 1970, there would be one million "viable" farms. This means that 20.6 percent of farms should have been "viable" farms in 1970.[1] However, the ratio of "viable" to total farms was only 6.6 percent in 1970 and declined further to 5.2 percent in 1980. It had been 8.6 percent in 1960. The government was very disappointed with the poor results of the Basic Agricultural Program. In 1973, the government shifted its policy from encouraging "viable" farms to encouraging "responsible" farms, which have at least one male farm worker younger than 60 years of age and working 150 days or more on his farm annually, and were to be responsible for the healthy growth of Japanese agriculture. These "responsible" farms made up one third of total farms and produced two thirds of the sector's output in 1973.

The high level of support for agriculture in Japan has increasingly been criticized by exporters. Judging from their age distribution, an increasing number of Japanese farmers will be retiring in the near future. They have to transfer their agricultural lands to other, younger farmers. Therefore, there will be increasing possibilities for these younger farmers to enlarge their farms. This is the background for the idea of playing catch-up with EC agriculture. According to the government's target for the program, declared in 1982, there will be 700,000 "responsible" farms in 1990. They will comprise 17 percent of total Japanese farms and will use 60 percent of total arable land. The average sizes of the largest 300,000 "responsible" farms are as follows:

Rice farms	Outside of Hokkaido	5 hectares
	In Hokkaido	10 hectares
Dairy farms	Outside of Hokkaido	25 milking cows (8 ha.)
	In Hokkaido	35 milking cows (35 ha.)
Beef farms	Outside of Hokkaido	70 cattle (5 ha.)
	In Hokkaido	100 cattle (20 ha.)

The number of "responsible" farms will decrease to 400,000 by the year 2000. However, there could be a fairly large number of 10-15 hectare rice farms and 20-35 hectare dairy farms. The above is the import of the catch-up program. The government has been stern in trying not to raise nominal producers' prices of various farm products during the past several years. It was expected that Japanese support levels will finally coverge with EC support levels since it was expected that the EC would have to increase its support prices.

The rice surplus has dominated the whole range of Japan's agricultural policy in recent years. Three successive good crops from 1967 to 1969 culminated in 7.2 million tons of stocks in 1970 which cost the government 1,000 billion yen to dispose of. In addition to surplus disposal, the government had to divert about 14 percent of the total paddy rice acreage in 1971-75 and about 23 percent in 1978-82 into other crops. Since rice is a sacred commodity in Japan and production of it was the most profitable among crops produced in Japan at that time, the government had to pay not only diversion payments but also various kinds of subsidies to those who grew non-rice crops such as wheat, soybeans, fodder crops and so forth on paddy fields. One effect of such diversion programs was the increase in wheat production from 1977 as shown in Figure JN-3. Another effect of the programs was the increase in the level of grain price supports from 1975 to 1980 as shown in Table 1. These and other effects of the crop diversion programs retarded, and will continue to retard, the swing of Japan's agricultural policy from the pole of increasing food supplies to the pole of increasing productivity significantly.

---

[1]The number of farms existing at the beginning of the 1960s was 6,005,000. To achieve one million "viable" farms by 1970, at least 1.2 million farms would have had to leave farming in the ten years 1960-70. 1,000,000 / (6,005,000 - 1,200,000) x 100 = 20.6.

Government Intervention at Border

The government support (price stabilization) programs have covered about 70 percent of total agricultural production. A major exception is fruits, none of which is subject to price support measures. In many cases the support levels are determined annually by very detailed (rigid) formulas such as the parity formula (wheat and barley), the cost of production and compensation formula (rice), etc. This necessitates various kinds of intervention. Moreover, *ad valorem* duties are less preferred than other forms of intervention because *ad valorem* duties are less effective in isolating domestic support prices from price fluctuations in the world market.

Besides moderate import duties, the following government interventions at the border are presently used in connection with domestic price supports for various commodities. Rice, wheat, flour, barley, sterilized fresh milk and cream, condensed milk, butter and tobacco leaves are subject to state-trading. Beef, oranges, processed cheese, peanuts and some juices (including orange juice) are subject to quota systems (residual quantitative import restrictions). Sugar is subject to a variable levy system that works when the c.i.f. price is lower than a certain level. Maize for non-feeding purposes is subject to a tariff quota system. Pork, ham and bacon are subject to sliding tariff rates. Soybeans, sugar, rapeseed and milk for processing are subject to deficiency payment systems.

Effects of Import Liberalization on Selected Commodities

As is made clear at the beginning of Chapter IV of the foregoing report, we are not advocating that levels of protection everywhere be zero. We are recommending that domestic agricultural programs must be made more market-oriented. However, in order to illustrate the magnitude of the possible effects on domestic agriculture of lowering levels of protection, the results of investigation into the effects of complete import liberalization are presented here.

There are two views in Japan concerning the effects of import liberalization on agricultural products. The first view, asserted during the final phase of the last U.S.-Japan trade negotiation on beef and oranges, is that even if Japan liberalizes imports of these commodities, the increase in imports will be small (about 500 million dollars), while at the same time these liberalizations will affect producers' incomes very seriously. This view is based on the assumption that price elasticities of both demand for and supply of these commodities are very small. Therefore, the first view is an observation of short-run effects. The second view agrees that in the short run agricultural import liberalization will have very serious economic effects on producers, and that agricultural land prices will decline. Sympathizers of the second view go on to assert, however, that with the decline in land prices, more efficient producers will use the agricultural land of less efficient producers, and the more efficient producers will further increase their efficiency. *In the long run* they will be competitive enough to compete with foreign exporters. This view assumes that imports of liberalized commodities will not increase very much in the long run, but may increase significantly *in the short run*. One advocate of this view quotes the Cost of Production of Rice Survey by the Ministry of Agriculture, Forestry and Fisheries (Figure JN-6). The survey shows that even at present land prices the most efficient producers (operating a 7 hectare farm in Northeast Japan) could survive even with a halved rice price. The advocate of this view also quotes the cost of producing rice for one of the most efficient farmers in Southwest Japan. The cost of producing rice on this farm is about two thirds that of the most efficient producers in Northeast Japan.

The price elasticity of demand for beef is 1.74, the biggest figure among food commodities. However, it is widely believed that the elasticity may be much smaller for a price change over a wide range. Using published estimates of coefficients of price elasticities of demand for foods, the probable effects of import liberalization on domestic use of selected foods are tentatively calculated in Table JN-2. Rice consumption will increase by 1.8 million tons. Beef consumption will be more than doubled. These figures contradict what Japanese usually are thinking about consumption of these commodities. Moreover, it should be noted that there may be substitution effects of increased rice and beef consumption on wheat, pork and chicken consumption. Wheat consumption would increase only 12,000 tons instead of 48,000 tons. Pork and chicken consumption would decrease 118 thousand tons and 115 thousand tons respectively. As for feed grains, there would be a decrease of 0.7 million tons. If beef imports increased more than 0.6 million tons, there would be a further decrease in domestic use of feed grains.

Our knowledge about price elasticities of supply for agricultural commodities is even poorer than our knowledge about price elasticities of demand. It is generally believed that Japanese producers are far less competitive in grain production than in factory-type production methods such as those used for pork, chicken, eggs, and greenhouse vegetables. Except for oranges, imports of various fruits are liberalized already. Therefore, it is

FIGURE JN-6

Economies of Scale in Rice Production in Northeast Japan

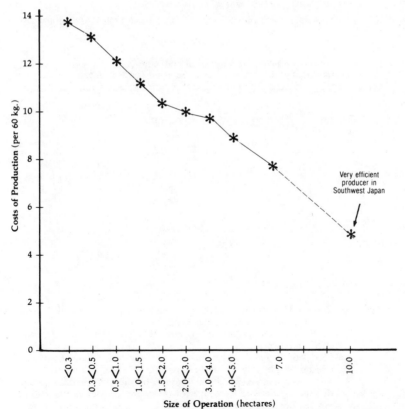

Size of Operation (hectares)

Source: National Institute of Research Advancement, "Formulating a Policy for Independent Japanese Agriculture, 1981" (Tokyo: National Institute for Research Advancement, in Japanese), p. 19.

believed that orange (*mikan*) production could be competitive in an import-liberalized economy. Beef and dairy products are in an intermediate position.

If imports of rice, wheat and barley are liberalized, producer prices of these products would decline by 77 percent, 75 percent and 80 percent respectively. There would be almost no producer of these products who could compete at these low prices. About 18 percent of the present cost of rice production is land rent. If rental of land becomes much cheaper, efficient 10 hectare rice farmers could produce rice at a cost equal to one quarter of the present cost. If there is a moderate import tariff, the situation would be somewhat better. There would be no such hope for domestic wheat and barley production.

Butter, nonfat dry milk and beef are more competitive than grains. Producer prices of butter, nonfat dry milk and beef would decline by about a half. There would be a small number of producers of these products who could compete at these low prices (and producers of higher quality beef, for example, could get higher prices). Unfortunately the number of these producers is not available. Moreover, recent developments in packing fresh milk make it possible to transport fresh milk to very distant places. The same can be said in the cases of peanuts, sugar and tobacco.

Consumer and Taxpayer Costs

Estimates of the consumer and taxpayer costs of Japanese support programs are shown in Table JN-3. Three significant points should be noticed:

• The levels of agricultural price supports to producers (NRP in Table 1) are higher than

TABLE JN-2

**Probable Effects of Import Liberalization on
Domestic Prices and Domestic Use of Selected Foods in Japan**

	Change in Consumer Price (percent)	Domestic Use in 1982 or 1983 (1,000 met. ton)	Changes in Domestic Use	
			(%)	(1,000 met. ton)
Rice: for direct consumption	− 75.8	6,535	+ 14.4	+941
for processing	− 51.6	953	+ 87.2	+834
Wheat	− 26.3	6,020	+ 0.8	+ 48
Barley	− 38.8	2,462	+ 1.2	+ 30
Peanuts	− 31.4	67	+ 48.6	+ 33
Butter	− 64.7	66	—	—
Nonfat dry milk	− 68.3	298	+ 2.7	+ 80
Beef	− 59.6	589	+103.7	+611
Sugar	− 50.4	3,200	− 10.6	−339
Tobacco	− 30.2	153	—	—

Note and sources: These effects are calculated by using constant price elasticities of demand for the commodities concerned. The coefficients of price elasticity of demand are taken from MAFF, *Demand Analysis, 1982* (1983) for rice and sugar; and from M. Sawada, "A Hierarchical Model of Demand and Food in Japan," *Journal of Rural Economics* (December 1984) for wheat, barley and beef. The coefficient for peanuts was calculated by Kenzo Hemmi, and the coefficient for nonfat dry milk is derived from that for cakes and cookies in the MAFF volume noted above.

excess consumer costs as a percentage of the value of domestic use at world prices. This is because for many commodities government support prices for producers are much higher than the domestic prices for consumers shown in Table JN-3. There appear to be two reasons for this. First, there are some deficiency payments to producers such as those for milk for processing, soybeans and rapeseeds. Even in the case of rice, government selling prices (consumer prices) are still lower than government purchase prices (producer prices), although the government has tried to reduce the difference. Second, rice does not compete with other grains in land use. Therefore, the rice self-sufficiency policy is possible without supporting producer prices of other grains such as maize. Although there is some production of dryland rice, these are the least rewarding areas, and rice production generally does not penetrate into dryland fields. (As explained at the end of the previous section, with the recent introduction of the rice diversion program, the government increased the support levels of wheat and barley.) Domestic use prices of wheat and barley are a weighted average of very high producer prices and low prices of imported grains which hold very large shares in domestic use.

- The rice and beef programs in combination take three fourths of the total excess consumer costs. The rice program takes almost all taxpayer costs.
- There were slight declines in the levels of producer supports between 1979 and 1983. This trend is also seen in the small decline both in excess consumer costs as a percentage of the value of domestic use at world prices and in taxpayer costs as a percentage of the same value. As seen in Table 1, government support levels have increased steadily from 1955 to 1980 (although there were slight declines in the levels of livestock supports from 1965 to 1970, and in the levels of grains supports from 1970 to 1975). These slight declines in consumer and taxpayer costs confirm the swing of government policy since 1980 from the pole of increasing food supplies (food security) toward increasing productivity.

It is generally assumed that deficiency payments are preferable to price supports as a way to protect producers. Between 1960 and 1970 the government budget for agriculture, forestry and fisheries increased more rapidly than the total Japanese government budget (Table JN-4). During this period, the producer price of rice had risen more rapidly than the consumer price of rice and the Food Control System swallowed huge amounts of government money. In 1970 the Food Control System took about half of the budget for agriculture, forestry and fisheries. There were 7.2 million tons of accumulated stocks of rice in 1970. Since then, the Japanese government has tried to reduce the taxpayer costs of the Food Control System, as shown in Table JN-4. Except for the year from 1973 to 1974, producer prices increased more slowly than consumer prices (Table JN-5). We can conclude that the Japanese government has tried to shift the costs of producer support from the taxpayers' shoulders to the consumers' shoulders. Especially in the last three or four years, the budget for agriculture, forestry and fisheries (and that for the Food Control System) has gone down in absolute terms. We wonder if this government effort will be reversed.

As shown in Table JN-3, about two thirds of the costs of support programs have been borne by consumers. If Japan can reduce this two thirds to one half, and if the costs of the Food Control System do not increase very much, the Japanese government can change almost all non-rice price support programs into deficiency payment systems. Of course, there is no doubt that the real core of prospects for modification of Japanese agricultural support policy lies in the possibility of productivity increases by rice producers, as pointed out in the *Report of the Japan-United States Economic Relations Group*.[2]

---

[2]*Report of the Japan-United States Economic Relations Group*, prepared for the President of the United States and the Prime Minister of Japan (Tokyo and Washington: January 1981), p. 85.

TABLE JN-3

**Costs of Farm Price Support and Income Stabilization Programs
to Consumers and Taxpayers in Japan,
1979 and 1983**

COMMODITY	DOMESTIC USE (thousand met. ton)	PRICE			VALUE OF DOMESTIC USE AT WORLD PRICES	EXCESS CONSUMER COSTS
		DOMESTIC	WORLD	DIFFERENCE		
		(thousand yen/ton)			(million yen)	
			1979			
Rice (I)[a]	6,535	277[c]	62	215	405,170	1,405,025
	953	139[c]	62	77	59,086	73,381
Rice (II)[a]	6,535	256[c]	62	194	405,170	1,267,790
	953	128[c]	62	66	59,086	62,898
Wheat[a]	5,337	57	42	15	224,154	80,055
Barley[a]	1,042	49	30	19	31,260	19,798
Other grains[a]	2,219	29	29	0	64,351	0
Soybeans	4,332	70	70	0	303,240	0
Peanuts	67	331	227	104	15,209	6,968
Other beans	445	119	119	0	512,955	0
Potatoes	4,965	67	67	0	332,052	0
Butter	66	1,110	392	718	25,872	47,388
Nonfat dry milk	298	420	133	287	125,160	85,526
Milk, fluid	3,905	101	101	0	394,405	0
Beef	589	1,202	587	615	345,743	362,235
Pork	1,641	724	724	0	1,188,084	0
Mutton	231	347	347	0	80,157	0
Chicken meat	1,162	410	410	0	476,420	0
Horse	94	466	466	0	43,804	0
Eggs	1,897	242	242	0	459,074	0
Sugar	3,200	127	63	64	201,600	204,800
Citrus[a]	3,864	72	72	0	278,208	0
Tobacco[b]	153	1,576	1,100	476	168,300	72,828

Value of domestic use at world prices (A)	5,566,004
Excess consumer costs	(I) 2,285,176; (II) 2,137,458
as percent of value of domestic use at world prices	(I) 41.1%; (II) 38.4%
Taxpayer costs (Food Control)	1,297,234[b] (1,072,800)
as percent of value of domestic use at world prices	23.3%
Total costs to consumers and taxpayers (B)	(I) 3,582,410; (II) 3,434,692
as percent of value of domestic use at world prices	(I) 64.4%; (II) 61.7%
Value of domestic use of commodities not included above (C)	2,904,600
A + C	8,470,604
B as percent of A + C	(I) 42.3%; (II) 40.5%

TABLE JN-3 (Continued)

**Costs of Farm Price Support and Income Stabilization Programs
to Consumers and Taxpayers in Japan,
1979 and 1983**

COMMODITY	DOMESTIC USE (thousand met. ton)	PRICE			VALUE OF DOMESTIC USE AT WORLD PRICES	EXCESS CONSUMER COSTS
		DOMESTIC	WORLD	DIFFERENCE		
		(thousand yen/ton)			(million yen)	
			1983			
Rice (I)[a]	6,923	342[c]	117	225	809,991	1,577,675
	890	178[c]	117	61	104,130	54,290
Rice (II)[a]	6,923	284[c]	117	167	809,991	1,156,141
	890	142[c]	117	25	104,130	22,250
Wheat[a]	5,408[e]	69	51	18	275,808	97,344
Barley[a]	1,096[e]	61	40	21	43,840	23,016
Other grains[a]	2,876[e]	36	36	0	103,536	0
Soybeans	4,550	70	70	0	31,850	0
Peanuts	49	330	226	104	11,074	5,096
Other beans	439	197	197	0	66,483	0
Potatoes	5,353	51	51	0	273,003	0
Butter	67[e]	1,340[e]	716[e]	624	47,972	41,808
Nonfat dry milk	303[e]	543[e]	294[e]	249	89,082	75,447
Milk, fluid	4,276	100	100	0	427,600	0
Beef	681[e]	1,099[e]	682[e]	417	464,442	283,977
Pork	1,625[e]	815[e]	815[e]	0	1,324,375	0
Mutton	117[e]	386[e]	386[e]	0	45,162	0
Chicken meat	1,306[e]	460[e]	460[e]	0	600,760	0
Horse	76[e]	552[e]	552[e]	0	41,952	0
Eggs	1,961[e]	338[e]	338[e]	0	662,818	0
Sugar	3,093[e]	139[e]	57[e]	82	176,301	253,626
Citrus[a]	3,237[e]	93[e]	93[e]	0	301,041	0
Tobacco[b]	137	1,729	1,388	341	190,156	46,717

Value of domestic use at world prices (A)	6,091,376
Excess consumer costs	(I) 2,412,279; (II) 1,958,705
as percent of value of domestic use at world prices	(I) 39.6%; (II) 32.2%
Taxpayer costs (Food Control)	1,120,710[b] (917,230)
as percent of value of domestic use at world prices	18.4%
Total costs to consumers and taxpayers (B)	(I) 3,532,989; (II) 3,079,415
as percent of value of domestic use at world prices	(I) 58.0%; (II) 50.6%
Value of Domestic Use of Commodities not included above (C)	2,914,700
A + C	9,006,076
B as percent of A + C	(I) 39.2%; (II) 34.2%

Notes for Table JN-3 on following page.

TABLE JN-4

Government Budget for Agriculture, Forestry and Fisheries in Japan
(billion yen)

	TOTAL GOVERNMENT BUDGET (A)	BUDGET FOR AGRICULTURE, FORESTRY AND FISHERIES (B)	BUDGET FOR FOOD CONTROL (C)	B AS % OF A	C AS % OF B
1960	1,765.2	166.9	29.0	9.5	17.4
1965	3,744.7	404.9	120.5	10.8	29.8
1970	8,213.1	992.1	488.1	12.1	49.2
1975	20,837.2	2,289.2	917.5	11.0	40.1
1980	43,681.4	3,776.5	1,032.1	8.6	27.3
1981	47,125.4	3,824.0	1,014.1	8.1	26.5
1982	47,562.1	3,820.7	1,005.4	8.0	26.3
1983	50,839.4	3,685.2	917.2	7.2	24.9
1984	50,627.2	3,459.7	813.2	6.8	23.5

TABLE JN-5

Rate of Increase in Rice Prices (%)

	PRODUCER PRICES	CONSUMER PRICES
1960-65	57.1	29.4
1965-70	26.5	32.1
1970-75	88.2	64.0
1975-80	13.5	30.2
1980-81	0.5	3.2
1981-82	1.1	3.9
1982-83	1.7	0.0
1983-84	2.2	3.7

Note: There was a 31.4% increase in the producer price from 1973 to 1974. If this increase is excluded, the average annual increase over the period was 8.15%, and 88.2% should be 40.8%.

Notes for Table JN-3.

[a]Consumption by producers themselves is not included in domestic use of rice and citrus. In the cases of wheat, barley and other grains, domestic use does not include grains fed to animals.

[b]Costs of the tobacco leaves program are not borne by consumers but by the government budget. Consumption of imported tobacco leaves (including those in cigarettes) is not included in domestic use figure. Therefore, in this line the cost figure in the final column has been tentatively included in taxpayer costs.

[c]There are two government selling prices of rice: one for direct consumption (upper price in each pair) and the other for processing (second in each pair). For each, two variations of domestic prices have been estimated (I and II), with different assumptions. Quality differences are more seriously considered in (II) than in (I).

[d]World prices are c.i.f. prices at the ports of imports plus reasonable handling charges at the ports. Import duties are not included here. In the cases of beef, pork and mutton, actual prices are converted into prices per ton of carcass. Moreover, for some commodities such as citrus, domestic prices are quoted as world prices since *mikan* prices were lower than c.i.f. prices of imported oranges. [e]1982

E. EFFECTS OF DOMESTIC PROTECTION
ON INTERNATIONAL PRICES

This part of the Appendix—which supports Section B of Chapter II of the foregoing report—briefly summarizes a number of studies that have been made of the effects of domestic farm programs and agricultural protection upon international market prices for some farm products. As noted in the above text, the trade interventions resulting from farm programs can affect both the level and variability of international market prices. Both effects have been considered by available studies.

It is necessary to note that the effects of the trade interventions in agriculture upon international market prices depend upon the level of protection that existed for the time period covered by the estimates. Some studies are based on the levels of protection that existed in 1975-77; others are based on 1978-80. Protection levels in the first period were significantly less than in the second one. As a result, the international price effects based on the 1975-77 period are the smaller of the two periods.

The studies undertaken by Tyers, Anderson and Chisholm at the Australian National University have been the most extensive. These studies have included five commodities or groups of commodities—rice, wheat, coarse grain, ruminant meat and nonruminant meat. In one exercise (Tyers, 1982) it was assumed that there was free trade in the principal market economies and the members of ASEAN. The results expressed in terms of projected prices, comparing a continuation of agricultural and trade policies (as of 1975-77) and free trade, are presented in Table E-1. The prices are the international trading prices expressed in 1970 US$ and are for different periods of adjustment—3 years, 8 years and 13 years. The reference prices are for continuation of 1975-77 interventions and the other prices are under the assumed liberalization.

The 1990 estimates, which allow sufficient time for all production and consumption adjustments to occur, indicate that the expected level of wheat and coarse grain prices under liberalization would differ from the prices under continuation of existing policies by less than 10 percent—actually by 7 percent for wheat and 4 percent for coarse grains. The increase for nonruminant meat was projected at 6 percent. The effect of liberalization on prices for ruminant meat was estimated to be very large, but part of this difference may be due to the difficulty of making appropriate adjustments for quality differences.

The results for rice are very interesting, with the projections indicating that liberalization would result in a fall in the price of about 20 percent by 1990. The explanation is that in a number of ASEAN countries rice prices are held below international market prices, especially for consumers but in some cases for producers as well. Thus if there were liberalization, rice consumption would fall and rice production would increase in the developing countries. These effects are anticipated to be larger than the reduction in production that would occur in Japan and the United States with the elimination of protection of rice.

Except for ruminant meat, the international market prices that prevail with the 1975-77 degree of protection depart rather little from the projected prices under trade liberalization. Unfortunately, the study does not include either dairy products or sugar, where the effects of liberalization upon international prices might be far greater.

The text of our report included a reference to estimates of the effects of the agricultural protection of the OECD countries upon the exports of farm products by the developing countries. These estimates, based upon 1975-77 levels of protection, involved projecting the price effects of the trade restrictions. Based on reducing protection levels by 50

TABLE E-1

Effects of Multilateral Agricultural Liberalization in the Principal Market Economies and ASEAN on International Trading Prices

		1980	1985	1990
Trading Prices, U.S.$ (1970)/ton				
Rice	Reference[a]	138	148	175
		(28)[c]	(34)	(29)
	Liberalization[b]	115	134	139
		(15)	(8)	(12)
Wheat	Reference	64	57	61
		(44)	(44)	(48)
	Liberalization	51	63	65
		(35)	(21)	(28)
Coarse Grain	Reference	49	49	53
		(24)	(22)	(21)
	Liberalization	47	54	55
		(14)	(15)	(20)
Ruminant Meat	Reference	411	448	532
		(16)	(20)	(17)
	Liberalization	735	769	799
		(4)	(5)	(4)
Nonruminant Meat	Reference	597	589	636
		(7)	(6)	(6)
	Liberalization	627	650	675
		(5)	(4)	(5)

[a]Projections based on continuation of agricultural policies as of 1975-77.

[b]Free trade, both internationally and domestically, assumed to prevail in Australia, Bangladesh, Canada, India, Indonesia, Japan, Republic of Korea, Malaysia, Pakistan, Philippines, Singapore, Sri Lanka, Thailand, United States and European Economic Community.

[c]Figures in parentheses are the coefficients of variation in percent.

Source: Rod Tyers, "Effects on ASEAN of Food Trade Liberalization in Industrial Countries," paper presented to the Second Western Pacific Food Trade Workshop, Jakarta, 22-23 August 1982. Coefficients of variation calculated from standard deviations given in the original.

percent, Valdes and Zietz (1980) obtained results comparable to those reported in Table E-1. Their study included 99 commodities, with the price increases resulting from reducing the barriers to trade reported for 47. There were only four commodities with price increases greater than 10 percent—and all of these were processed products: roast coffee, cocoa paste and powder, malt and wine. Other price increases were 2 percent for maize, 4 percent for wheat, 8 percent for raw sugar, 7 percent for beef and 9 percent for pork. The degree of protection for sugar in 1975-77 was much lower.

Ulrich Koester (1982), using the model and data bases developed by Valdes and Zietz, estimated the effect of removing the grain protection by the European Community upon the level of international market prices for grain. The projected increases in world grain market prices ranged from less than 1 percent for millet and sorghum to almost 20 percent for oats. For wheat the projected increase was 9.6 percent and for maize, 2.2 percent. The price increase for barley was projected at 14.3 percent. If the grains are weighted by the value of world exports in 1975-77, the average increase in price would have been 6.7 percent.

Maurice Schiff (1983) estimated a model of the world wheat market, based on econometric estimates of his own. Free trade was assumed for the European Community, the United States, Canada, Australia, Japan, and Argentina. The model included estimates of the wheat trade functions of the USSR and the rest of the world for continuation of existing policies. He estimates that if there had been free trade in wheat in the designated countries from 1964 to 1978 the average increase in world wheat prices would have been 15 percent. He also estimates that if there had been free trade in the European Community only, with all other countries continuing their actual policies, the world market price of wheat for the same period would have been 17 percent higher. This result may seem somewhat surprising until it is remembered that during most of the years included in the analysis the major exporters, especially the United States and Canada, had limited the output of wheat by domestic supply management programs. If there had been universal free trade, exports of wheat by the major exporters would have been somewhat higher than they actually were.

Stefan Tangerman and Wolfgang Korstitz (1982) estimated the effects of trade liberalization on the beef sector. They estimated the implicit tariff equivalent of the restraints on trade that existed during 1977-79. Elasticities of supply and demand were also estimated. With this information plus the actual levels of production and consumption of beef in each country or region, changes in production, consumption and net trade were estimated for reductions in the implicit tariffs of 25, 50 and 100 percent. They estimate that with full trade liberalization the international market price for beef would increase by 47 percent; this is almost identical to the 50 percent increase projected by Tyers.

One very interesting result is that no one of the three degrees of reduction of the implicit tariffs would have any noticeable effect upon domestic prices of beef in the United States or Canada. The reason for this rather striking result is that the increase in world market prices would be approximately equal to the reduction in the implicit tariff for each of the three cases—25, 50 or 100 percent. For example, if the United States reduced its implicit tariff by 50 percent, this would have amounted to a decrease in the tariff by $230 per ton (slaughter weight). However, if all countries reduced their implicit tariffs by 50 percent, the world price would increase by $220 per ton. For the European Community a reduction of its implicit tariff of 118 percent by 50 percent would have resulted in a decrease in the domestic price of 15 percent. The decline in the domestic price in Japan was projected to be 28 percent or $163 per ton.

Roy Allen, Claudia Dodge, and Andrew Schmitz (1983) arrive at a much more modest estimate of the effect of the voluntary export constraints for beef on beef prices in the

United States. For 1976/77, when there were voluntary restraints on beef exports to the United States, the U.S. price of frozen boneless beef was increased by about $85 per ton or about 8 percent of the free trade price. However, the price increase for all U.S. beef would be significantly smaller than the estimated 8 percent since beef of the quality that is imported accounts for no more than a quarter of U.S. beef consumption. An interesting result of the study was that the average price received by the exporters was slightly higher than it would have been under free trade. Under the voluntary quotas the exporters realized the price gain from the reduced level of U.S. imports. It may be noted that there were no voluntary restraints in effect during 1980, 1981 and 1982 though such restraints were imposed for the second half of 1983.

Tyers and Chisholm (1985) extended their study to include protection during the 1978-80 period. Due to the increased protection, the elimination of all protection in the long run would result in international market price increases of 20 percent for wheat, 16 percent for feed grains, 27 percent for ruminant meat and 2 percent for nonruminant meat. Rice prices were projected to increase by 6 percent. A projection for a reduction of protection by 50 percent from the 1978-80 level was made. The increases in international market prices were quite similar to the earlier projections based on 1975-77 protection levels—12 percent for wheat, 7 percent for coarse grains, 9 percent for ruminant meat and 1 percent for nonruminant meat. The price of rice was projected to decline by 3 percent.

The trade intervention policies not only affect the average level of international market prices but also influence the variability of prices. The figures in parentheses in Table E-1 are measures of the price variability under current policies and free trade. The measure is the coefficient of variation, which is in percentage terms and represents the relationship between the standard deviation of prices and the average price. For wheat, rice and ruminant meat the estimates indicate that current policies have substantially increased the variability of international market prices. For coarse grains and nonruminant meat the current policies have had little effect.

The much greater variability of international market prices under current policies than under free trade results from the nature of agricultural protection that prevails in many countries. Agricultural protection *per se* need not result in increasing price variability in international markets (and in the countries where international prices are directly reflected in domestic prices). It is the form of protection that causes the increased variability. Protection of agriculture that functions by stabilizing domestic prices through varying imports and exports of commodities destabilizes international market prices. It does so through using import and export changes to meet any variations in domestic supply and demand and by preventing internal price changes from absorbing at least part of the variability.

Consider the following example. A country has a fixed price of $100 per ton for grain, average use is 55,000,000 tons and average production is 50,000,000 tons. The price of $100 is maintained by varying the amount imported with average annual imports being 5 million tons. In one year production is 45 million tons and imports are increased by 5 million tons to 10 million tons. The internal price remains at $100. In the next year production is 55 million tons and there are no imports since none are required to keep the price at $100 if demand has remained unchanged. As this example indicates, all of the variability in domestic production is imposed upon the international market. None of the variability is absorbed by changing domestic use; since the price remains at $100 the users have no incentive to change. Nor are producers encouraged to increase their production in the year following the short crop. In effect, the country achieves domestic price stability by exporting instability through varying the imports to exactly offset the production departures from the average.

REFERENCES

Roy Allen, Claudia Dodge, and Andrew Schmitz, "Voluntary Restraints as Protection Policy: The U.S. Beef Case," *American Journal of Agricultural Economics*, 65, No. 2 (May 1983), pp. 291-96.

Kym Anderson, "Economic Growth, Comparative Advantage and Agricultural Trade," *Review of Marketing and Agricultural Economics*, 5, No. 3 (December 1983).

Kym Anderson and Rodney Tyers, "European Community's Grain and Wheat Policies and U.S. Retaliation: Effects on International Prices, Trade, and Welfare," unpublished paper, Department of Economics, Research School of Pacific Studies, Australian National University, Canberra, revised October 1983.

Anthony H. Chisholm and Rodney Tyers, "Agricultural Protection and Market Insulation Policies: Applications of a Dynamic Multi-sectoral Model," in *New Developments in Applied General Equilibrium Analysis*, edited by J. Whalley and J. Piggott (Cambridge: Cambridge University Press, 1985).

Ulrich Koester, *Policy Options for the Grain Economy of the European Community: Implications for Developing Countries*, Research Report 35 of the International Food Policy Research Institute (Washington, D.C.: November 1982).

Maurice Schiff, "Information, Expectations and Policies: A Study of the World Wheat Market," Ph.D. dissertation, The University of Chicago, 1983.

Stefan Tangerman and Wolfgang Korstitz, *Protectionism in the Livestock Sector with Particular Reference to the International Beef Trade* (Göttingen: Institut für Agrarökonomie der Universität Göttingen, 1982).

Rod Tyers, "Effects on ASEAN of Food Trade Liberalization in Industrial Countries," paper presented to the Second Western Pacific Food Trade Workshop, Jakarta, 22-23 August 1982.

Alberto Valdes, "Agricultural Protectionism: The Impact on LDCs," *Ceres* (November-December 1982), pp. 13-18.

Alberto Valdes and Joachim Zietz, *Agricultural Protection in OECD Countries: Its Cost to Less-Developed Countries*, Research Report 21 of the International Food Policy Research Institute (Washington, D.C.: December 1980).

F. RELATIVE FARM PRICES AND
RATES OF DECLINE IN FARM EMPLOYMENT

As Section C of Chapter III of the foregoing report states, if one compares the level of prices received by farmers across countries with the annual rates of decline in farm employment—data set out in the following two tables—one finds no significant relationship. High farm prices are not associated with low rates of decline and relatively low farm prices are not associated with high rates of decline in farm employment.

TABLE F-1

Prices Received by Farmers in Major Industrial Countries
($ per metric ton)

	1970		1979	
	WHEAT	COARSE GRAIN	WHEAT	COARSE GRAIN
Belgium	100	86	212	214
Denmark	—	62	224	214
France	84	75	232	214
Germany	99	89	274	247
Italy	110	93	231	210
Netherlands	102	—	212[a]	202[a]
United Kingdom	74	68	160	—
Ireland	76	—	—	181
Canada	61	—	117	100
Japan	162	131	770	582
United States	48	52	118	95

[a]1978.

TABLE F-2

Annual Rates of Decline in Farm Employment, 1955-79
(percent per year)

	1955-60	1960-70	1970-79
European Community	−3.2	−4.6	−3.4
Belgium	−3.7	−4.9	−4.6
Denmark	−2.1	−3.1	−2.7
France	−3.7	−3.7	−4.6
Germany	−3.3	−4.6	−4.8
Ireland	−2.5	−3.0	−3.1
Italy	−3.2	−5.8	−2.2
Netherlands	−2.7	−3.4	−1.8
United Kingdom	−2.5	−3.8	−1.0
Canada	−3.6	−2.7	−0.7
Japan	−2.6	−4.0	−4.1
United States	−3.3	−4.5	−0.5

Source: OECD publications.